If my life served only to com
would be well lived. Why? I h
network of healing initiatives from Cambodia to the inner cities and I am in awe of the works of Jesus in our day. Many wonderful books have been written but this one stands out. Set against the darkest backdrop of human depravity, Rhiannon's story, like Corrie Ten Boom's in the last generation, is profoundly powerful. It should be read by everyone. *Fire Lilies* is brilliant yet accessible to all. The stories are recounted with childlike simplicity yet contain transforming wisdom. Above all, the true nature of God's love is demonstrated. These pages will fill you with hope, understanding and joy.

John Dawson
Founder, International Reconciliation Coalition
President Emeritus, Youth With A Mission

Fire Lilies is a powerful story of Rhiannon's life and work. She has worked in the darkest places of the world; following Jesus, the bright Morning Star who heralds the ending of the dark night and the hope of a new day. Listening for His guidance, she has become a shining star for Him. It is a delight to read the text, see the pictures and marvel at the wonderful work she has initiated and transmitted to several faithful witnesses.

Josiane André
Co-founder of Medair

Rhiannon Lloyd, "Our Rhiannon". I met Rhiannon Lloyd in 1995 during a seminar for church leaders, one year after the genocide against the Tutsis. We were all searching for a healing balm for the wounded hearts of our people. Rhiannon later joined us in African Evangelistic Enterprise and she developed *Healing the Wounds of Ethnic Conflict*, a seminar that proved to be the answer we had been looking for. Read *Fire Lilies* and join Rhiannon on that search for an elixir of inner healing. Follow her in Liberia, Rwanda, Congo, Kenya and other places of suffering and grief. Meet those people who have been tried in the furnace of pain and healed at the foot of the cross, beautiful "fire lilies" that bloomed after a fire. You, too may be challenged to become one.

Rev. Dr. Antoine Rutayisire
Senior Pastor, Remera Anglican Church
Author *Faith Under* Fire, *Stories of Christian Bravery During the Genocide* and *Reconciliation is My Lifesty*le
Former Vice-Chairman, National Unity and Reconciliation Commission (1999-2011)

Rhiannon's life and experiences in the nations will reveal the heart of God to you in fresh, astonishing ways. God has trans-formation experiences for you as you read His story in the nations. What He has done for others, He will do for you. This book holds keys to His heart, and will be read by future generations.

Fawn Parish
People Developer, Author/Speaker
International Reconciliation Coalition/Reignbridge

Fire Lilies is an authentic story of a personal, spiritual and social journey over a lifetime. As Rhiannon vividly tells us about her life's ups and downs, we clearly see how the spiritual keys she discovered have been externalized and used as steps towards healing for individuals and communities around the world. We first got to know Rhiannon in the YWAM DTS and counselling school in the UK, and later we worked together for a great many years, predominantly in East Africa in communities devastated by genocide, civil unrest, and all kinds of injustice. We have stood alongside Rhiannon and personally witnessed reconciliation and healing taking place where humanly speaking there was no hope. Millions have been reached with the tools presented in *Fire Lilies*, filling us all with awe and amazement for how God changes people!

Today, it is still a privilege for us to continue working with many of the national leaders Rhiannon discipled and see the fruit continue multiplying. We whole heartedly recommend *Fire Lilies* as an incredible story worth reading to see how God can use anyone, even one single woman from Wales, to do great things for His Kingdom around the world.

Dr. Erik Spruyt
Director, Le Rucher Ministries

Rhiannon has uniquely been able to identify with the pain and trauma others have experienced – even out of situations of war and consequent loss. Whether through personal trials and illnesses, struggles and questions – through to the way that God can change nations. It's a remarkable story.

I have on a few occasions journeyed with Rhiannon. I have watched her identify with the woundedness of others, admired her spirit, appreciated the depth and creativity of her teaching, identified with her as a reconciler, prayed, laughed, and cried with her. I pray you will too, as you read this human, yet godly, story of repentance, forgiveness, and reconciliation. This is not only about Rhiannon, it is also about God.

Brian Mills
Author, International Prayer Council, Senior Leader

FIRE LILIES

FINDING HOPE IN UNEXPECTED PLACES

Dr. Rhiannon Lloyd

www.healingthenations.co.uk

This book is published by Healing the Nations Publishing.

Email: admin@healingthenations.co.uk

Copyright © 2021, 2023 by Dr Rhiannon Lloyd. All rights reserved.

Permission is granted to use brief excerpts from this book for review and teaching purposes. Please contact Healing the Nations for information and other permissions to use the contents of this book.

Scripture quotations taken from The Holy Bible, New International Version® NIV® Copyright © 1973 1978 1984 2011 by Biblica, Inc.™ Used by permission. All rights reserved worldwide.

Scripture quotations taken from the Amplified® Bible (AMP), Copyright © 2015 by The Lockman Foundation. Used by permission. www.lockman.org

Scripture quotations taken from The Message Bible are used with permission of the publisher, NavPress Publishing Group.

Cover illustration, design, and formatting by Mark Pierce, www.revelator.co.uk

The photographs in the Why Fire Lilies section are Meet the Fire Lily by Callan Cohen and are licenced under CC-BY-SA 3.0

The other photographs have been taken by friends and colleagues and are published with permissions.

The paintings in chapters 15 and 22 were painted in Rwanda and are published with permission from Rabagirana Ministry.

The authors of the songs and hymns have been included in the text.

ISBN 978-1-7399228-2-5

eISBN 978-1-7399228-1-8

Library of Congress Control Number 2021916870

An audio version of *Fire Lilies* is also available.

To my special sister Gwenda

and

to all the heroes who received the message

and began to live it

without whom this book

could not have been written.

CONTENTS

Glossary CHRISTIAN ORGANISATIONS	i
Preface WHY FIRE LILIES?	iii
Introduction AN ORDINARY PERSON	v
Chapter 1 THE BRIDGE	1
Chapter 2 DESIGNED BY A MASTER CRAFTSMAN	5
Chapter 3 WHERE ON EARTH HAVE I LANDED?	15
Chapter 4 ON BEING WELSH	23
Chapter 5 FACING MY INNER STRUGGLES	33
Chapter 6 DISCOVERING GOD AS THE REDEEMER OF EVERYTHING	41
Chapter 7 MORE EXPERIENCES OF PREPARATION	51
Chapter 8 LESSONS LEARNT IN LIBERIA	63
Chapter 9 INVITATION TO RWANDA	77

Chapter 10	MEETING CHRISTIAN LEADERS IN KIGALI	85
Chapter 11	FINDING HEALING AT THE CROSS	93
Chapter 12	THE *HEALING THE WOUNDS OF ETHNIC CONFLICT WORKSHOP* IS BORN	103
Chapter 13	THE HWEC WORKSHOPS DEVELOPE	117
Chapter 14	MULTIPLYING THE MINISTRY	131
Chapter 15	FINDING GOD AS A LOVING FATHER	143
Chapter 16	SHOCKING FORGIVENESS	151
Chapter 17	THE CHALLENGE OF REPENTANCE	161
Chapter 18	INVITATION TO SOUTH AFRICA	173
Chapter 19	NEW CREATIVE IDEAS IN SOUTH AFRICA	181
Chapter 20	THE MESSAGE SPREADS TO CONGO	199
Chapter 21	AND TO KENYA	215
Chapter 22	AND TO THE WORLD…	225
AFTERWORD		243
AND FINALLY, AS THE JOURNEY CONTINUES		255
Appendix 1 SUGGESTIONS FOR PERSONAL OR GROUP REFLECTION		263
Appendix 2 HEALING HEARTS, TRANSFORMING NATIONS		271
Appendix 3 ACKNOWLEDGEMENTS		275

Glossary
CHRISTIAN ORGANISATIONS

African Evangelistic Enterprise (AEE), www.aeerwanda.ngo, is part of the larger organisation: African Enterprise (AE), www.africanenterprise.com. AE currently operates in 10 African countries, seeking to bring the Gospel to their country, in word and deed, in partnership with the church.

EFICOR, www.eficor.org, is a national Christian relief and development organisation in India engaged in disaster response, sustainable development and training & capacity building programs.

Le Rucher Ministries, www.lerucher.org, is based near Geneva, and aims to equip people to impact a needy world. As well as focusing on debriefing and community development, it also supports ethnic reconciliation ministries in several countries.

Medair, www.medair.org, is an international humanitarian organisation inspired by Christian faith to relieve human suffering in some of the world's most remote and devastated places. It is based in Switzerland.

Operation Mobilisation (OM), ww.om.org, is a Christian missionary organisation founded by George Verwer to mobilise young people to live and share the Gospel of Jesus Christ.

Rabagirana Ministries, www.rabagirana.org, is based in Rwanda. Their passion is to see Rwanda become a model of lasting peace, unity and light to the nations to the glory of God. Their main focus is ethnic reconciliation, community development and servant leadership.

Resonate Global Mission, www.resonateglobalmission.org, has a vision to bring the Gospel to people, neighbourhoods, comm-unities, churches, and the world to embolden them in participating in God's mission and faithfully proclaiming and living out the good news of Jesus.

Tearfund, www.tearfund.org, is an international Christian relief and development agency based in Teddington, UK. Tearfund currently works in around 50 countries, with a primary focus on supporting those in poverty and providing disaster relief for disadvantaged communities.

Youth with a Mission (YWAM), www.ywam.org, is a global movement, full of mainly young people, driven by a passion to know God and make Him known.

Preface

WHY FIRE LILIES?

In my mind's eye I saw the whole land covered with ashes and I wept at the sense of desolation and despair. I was in Rwanda, praying with some friends on my second visit there, very soon after the 1994 genocide against the Tutsi. Then, as we prayed together, the picture began to change and I saw beautiful red flowers growing out of the ashes. I told God that I was going to believe for beauty to come from Rwanda's ashes.

A few years later, I was in South Africa and a friend and I planned to go walking near Cape Point. On arrival we discovered there had been a bushfire and the whole hillside was covered in ashes. Thinking this would not be a pleasant place to walk, we turned away, but then heard people calling us from the hilltop. 'Have you seen the fire lilies?' They explained to us that these are South African flowers which only bloom after a fire. The seeds may remain underground for many years, but when there is a fire above ground the heat causes the seeds to crack open and begin growing. 'Go and see,' they said.

So up the hillside we scrambled and, sure enough, there they were. And they were red. With tears in my eyes, I told my friend, 'I know the names of these flowers! They're Anastase and Joseph and Devota and Deborah and Judith and Abednego… my precious friends in Rwanda who have been through the fire and emerged from it beautiful.'

Fire lilies from Cape Peninsula, South Africa, January 2016
Meet the Fire Lily by Callan Cohen licenced under CC-BY-SA 3.0

Introduction

AN ORDINARY PERSON

I am an ordinary person with weaknesses and struggles, who discovered that God can use everything for His glory. Nothing is wasted with Him. He can turn all our trials into gold that can bless someone else. He can even redeem our weaknesses and sufferings and turn them into something life-giving. No one could have been more surprised than I was.

I spent years mentally struggling with God's character – can one really believe that He is good and loving when one goes through suffering and injustice? And what about the state of the world? I never imagined that God would use me to be a hope-bearer in some of the most tragic places on earth. Yet it was those very struggles that God used to unlock thousands of wounded hearts and bring hope of healing.

I never wanted to write a book about my story. That's because I believe that the heroes are the ones who have accepted this message about healing, forgiveness and reconciliation, and have run with it, often at great personal cost. I was happy to tell their story, but not mine.

That changed when I attended a conference and a young man who had never met me and knew nothing about me, approached me, saying God had drawn his attention to my hands. He felt God was saying, 'There are stories in you that the world needs to hear, so get writing.' So this was written as an act of obedience.

REDEMPTION

These are stories of redemption. For a long time, I didn't under-stand the meaning of that word, thinking it meant the same as salvation. The word 'saviour' describes someone who performs the act of rescuing, being *brought* back from death to life, in the fullest sense, but redeeming describes everything being '*bought*' back'. And not only that, but Jesus bought it all back with interest.

Jesus paid the full price to buy back *all* that Satan, the Thief, has stolen from us. I don't think I could ever have gone into some of the darkest, saddest places on earth if that had not been revealed to me. Everything is redeemable. There is no greater hope than this.

My work has not been without its difficulties, challenges and pain, but what a privilege it has been and still is, to see God healing and transforming wounded hearts, some full of hatred and turning them into beautiful fire lilies. It has been worth it all.

INTRODUCTION – AN ORDINARY PERSON

HOPE

These are stories of hope. Hope that nothing is wasted with God. He can use all our experiences, positive and negative, to accomplish the work He desires to do through us. He has given us the gifts and personality we need to fulfil His purpose. As you read these stories my desire is that you may have increased hope that God can use even painful parts of your history to bless someone else.

HEALING

Healing is a major emphasis in this book. The good news is that all our inner wounds can be healed, even those caused by genocide. God is just as concerned about our woundedness as He is with our sinfulness and has made provision in the cross to deal with both. This is another significant reason to have hope.

GOD'S LEADING

These stories show how God can lead us when we're not even aware of being led. I always struggled with a feeling of inadequacy about hearing God's voice and receiving His guidance. How do we know if we are really in His will? I should perhaps point out here that, although in many places I describe God revealing things to me, I usually only recognised this in hindsight. I have never had any dramatic, supernatural guidance.

God's prompting was simply a thought that came into my head which I acted on. Looking back, I was able to see the fruit of that and could only conclude that it had been God guiding me all along.

I have gradually discovered that God speaks to us individually according to our personalities and gifting. Having spent so many years complaining that I never hear God's voice, I have had to conclude that I do hear God's voice, but it usually comes through my natural thoughts. Most often, I have simply walked through the next door that opened, with no idea about where that was leading.

GOD'S CHARACTER

I want you to see in these stories the amazing beauty and wonderful qualities of God's character, His heart. He is totally trustworthy and very much at work in our broken, sinful world. Satan is the 'father of lies' who constantly seeks to poison our thinking about God's character and will. Yet, as Tozer puts it, in *The Roots of the Righteous*:

The truth is that God is the most winsome of all beings and His service one of unspeakable pleasure.

God is doing beautiful and wonderful things all the time and we only hear of a few of them. But one day we will hear them all and marvel and worship. God is truly awesome. My prayer is that this will come across most clearly and powerfully.

This is my personal life story, describing how God used me to bring about the unexpected birth, growth and expansion of an international work now called Healing Hearts, Transforming Nations, (initially called Healing the Wounds of Ethnic Conflict). I invite you to join me on this journey.

In Appendix One you will find some suggestions for personal or group reflection for each chapter.

Chapter One

THE BRIDGE

When I saw the rope bridge swinging precariously over a deep rushing river probably infested with crocodiles, I was aghast. We were expected to cross *this*?

It was April 2007 and we were in the northeast of the Democratic Republic of Congo. My Swiss friend Cathy and I were conducting a training session in Healing and Ethnic Reconciliation in Nyankunde, a town ravaged by a 10-year civil war that had only recently come to an end. It was an hour's drive from Bunia, where we were based. Because of the war, we had not been able to travel outside Bunia in previous visits. 'We're taking you to a tourist site as a small detour on the way,' our friends from the local team told us. We were a little puzzled when told we should wear our best clothes, but we didn't question it.

The vehicle stopped in a rural area and we were led along a long path through the bushes towards a river. As we approached, we heard singing from the hillside on the other side of the river. Looking up, we noticed a big crowd of people waving branches. 'What's going on there?' we asked. The team smiled. 'They've come to meet you,' they said. 'Some have walked for six hours to thank you for bringing the message of peace into our country. This message has stopped the war. That's the centre where the local militia used to meet.'

Our hearts were full of awe and thankfulness – until we saw the rope bridge. But whatever our hesitation and fear, we had to cross it to meet these people. There was much laughter from the local team as we struggled in long skirts, sometimes on all fours, to negotiate the flimsy swinging bridge of rope and branches, whilst trying not to look at the raging river below…

The crowd were pushing their way toward the bridge to welcome us, singing, and waving branches. *Is this how the Queen feels?* I wondered, as I kept waving. The meeting that followed was so moving as we heard one testimony after another of how the message of healing and reconciliation in our workshops had changed hearts and caused warring factions to stop fighting. The local chief gave a speech and thanked us for helping to bring peace to their region.

Finally, he asked if there was any way we could help finance a repair of the bridge as it was unsafe. This was the last thing we wanted to hear before having to negotiate it once again to get back to our vehicle, especially as we were now carrying seven live hens and a basket of eggs that had been given us!

THE BRIDGE

How on earth did I, a little Welsh woman, find myself in such a situation? I never planned to do anything like this. Much later I discovered that God's planning for this had started before I was even born...

The bridge

Chapter Two

DESIGNED BY A MASTER CRAFTSMAN

'Who am I? What has made me *me*?' These were questions I often pondered. I struggled with low self-esteem, so often comparing myself negatively with others. I really envied those who were calm and serene and seemed to take everything in their stride. Why hadn't God made me physically beautiful? I remember sitting on my bed at university, feeling like an empty eggshell. Depending on the company I was keeping at the time, there were different faces painted on the outside, but was there anything of value on the inside?

Proverbs 8 speaks of Someone called Wisdom, who was present at the creation – described as a craftsman, an architect, a master craftsman, delighting in mankind. The Bible calls Jesus the wisdom of God (1 Corinthians 1:24); John 1:2-3 declares He was with God in the beginning and that through Him, all things were made.

I am now convinced that we were designed by a Master Craftsman long before we were even conceived, so that each of us would become a unique person with personality, gifts and skills exactly corresponding to what God had in mind for our lives. For some time I had been marvelling at the way I was led into a ministry that I love and which is really 'me', though at the time I was completely unaware of what He was doing. I felt God responded by saying, 'I know your size.'

I believe we are most fulfilled when we are free to be the people He designed us to be: *'I won't lay anything ill-fitting on you'* (Matthew 11:28-30; 'The Message'). Though, of course, none of us can adequately respond to any call of God to us personally unless He equips and sustains us. We can't do it simply with our own 'natural resources'.

Looking back at my early life, I can see a pattern emerging. Even as a young child, I was an 'ideas person', 'Let's try this.' I loved music, drama and symbolism, and was familiar with taking initiative. 'If no one else is going to do this, then I will.' I would rally the children in my village to produce concerts and dramas for our long-suffering parents and neighbours who were appreciative and encouraging. We didn't need scripts – I encouraged us all to be spontaneous and follow our hearts, but I also had high standards and wanted everything done as well as possible.

I loved public speaking too, and was chosen both in primary and secondary schools to give speeches on behalf of the pupils at special occasions. In secondary school, I was the youngest person selected as part of a debating team for an inter-school radio competition. In our school drama competitions, I wrote, directed and played the main parts in the dramas and usually we won. All this was great fun – I enjoyed it far more than lessons. But I realise now that God was preparing me for His future plan for me, although I didn't yet know Him. God sanctifies our natural gifts to use for the furtherance of His Kingdom.

Also, for as long as I can remember, I had an interest in other nations. I picked this up from my parents. My father had travelled around Europe a fair bit before marrying late, and loved talking about the different countries he had visited. My mother played a significant part in the early days of 'Urdd Gobaith Cymru' – a Welsh league of youth which aimed to be the hope of the nation. Their motto was 'I will be faithful to Wales, to my fellow man and to Christ.' They produced a radio programme called 'Dydd Ewyllys Da' (Day of Goodwill) where Welsh children would deliver goodwill messages to children in other countries who would respond in like manner. This was one of the highlights of my year.

An international Eisteddfod (a festival of music and dance competitions) was held annually in the North Wales town of Llangollen. It was also designed to promote goodwill between nations and appreciation of other cultures.

Our school choir would have a day trip there and I loved it, hearing different styles of singing and seeing national dances. I suggested we have a competition among ourselves as to who could collect the most autographs from different countries, being determined that I would win. I became excited at the thought of travelling to other countries and learning about their cultures.

CHILDHOOD PAIN

However, my childhood also included much pain. My sister Gwenda (my only sibling) was born two years after me and as she grew up it became apparent that all was not well. She didn't seem able to grasp things and would often be very frustrated and aggressive. She was seen by doctors but no one understood the nature of her problem. Things became so bad at times that she had to be admitted to a mental hospital for our safety. In those days there was no provision in our region for those with learning disabilities.

From what I know now, it seems that when she caught measles at the age of four years, she also had encephalitis, which caused an arrest in her emotional and cognitive development, some coordination difficulties and mild epilepsy. Possibly there was also a family history of autism.

Gwenda and me, 2010

My reaction was to see her as a burden, a millstone round our necks. I was ashamed of having a sister who was different and badly behaved, especially when people stared at us. I'm sure that I added to her feelings of woundedness and rejection.

It was a long struggle to accept her as anything but a problem, although through it I developed an awareness of family needs and problems that may be largely hidden from the community.

Now I see her as God's gift to me – a precious sister and friend. I have learnt so much through relating to her – especially the need to try to understand her, seeking to 'put myself in her skin'. I would ask myself, 'What does it feel like to be Gwenda?' and tried to communicate clearly and simply, checking she had really understood. These skills would prove invaluable later in my life.

When I was 11 years old my mother developed a severe form of rheumatoid arthritis and before long was confined to a wheelchair. She was a lovely person, with a love of culture, a natural musician, creative, writing poetry, children's stories and dramas. She was gracious towards everyone, forgiving and honouring, hating conflict, always seeking peace. But she was also quite shy, with low self-esteem, not comfortable doing anything in public.

She had a heart for the outcast. I well remember that at Christmas she wanted to give cards and gifts to those in the village who would least expect to receive one. But it had to be done secretly and anonymously. Being sent on a mission to leave a card and gift at someone's door, ring the bell and run away as fast as I could, was maybe the greatest joy of Christmas. In her youth, my mother had written some lovely hymns, dedicating her life to the Lord, but because of a general lack of Biblical teaching in the church, had not grown in her experience of God.

Having a mother who was crippled and in constant pain was a great weight on me as I loved her very much, but she showed great fortitude in her suffering. I never heard her complain. Nurses who came to care for her said that they received more from her than they gave. She died suddenly when I was in my early twenties and I cried myself to sleep for many months.

My parents' wedding

My father was a lot older than my mother and found personal relationships very difficult. He was a scientist, a clever man, who was interested in world affairs. He didn't believe in militarism, saying it didn't solve anything and that made a lasting impression on me. He loved drama and had a good sense of humour. He was faithful, determined and persevered in the face of difficulties, in spite of his own lack. I now think he probably had a form of autism. Consequently, he was unable to support any of us emotionally, although he sought to meet our physical and educational needs to the best of his ability. The result is that I soon found myself in a parenting role, parenting everyone.

Although I had grown up proud of being Welsh, with a strong sense of identity and love for our rich culture, there was also a deep-seated pain associated with my 'Welsh-ness'. I'll say more on that aspect in another chapter, especially on the way that God healed and transformed me, as that has been very significant in the reconciliation work I do.

FINDING A PERSONAL FAITH

I was shocked when, towards the end of secondary school, a friend told me she had 'become a Christian' and that I needed it too. Did she think I was a pagan? I fought hard against her arguments. After all, I had grown up in a religious family in a religious culture. I attended church regularly and was a Sunday school teacher, but God seemed very distant. No one talked of a personal relationship with God and going to church felt like a cultural activity, something to preserve our 'Welsh-ness.'

A few months later, I attended a Christian youth rally with her and experienced young people like me appearing to have an intimate relationship with a God who was very real and active. After a sleepless night, I told Jesus I wanted to 'sign up' and become a real Christian, whatever that meant. I had very little understanding of the Gospel at that time, but received assurance that Jesus had heard and accepted me and I was filled with joy.

I tried to evangelise everyone around me, telling them they needed Jesus too and understandably experienced a lot of opposition from all quarters.

The headmistress called me into her room, expressing great concern for my sudden religious fervour. 'You had better let go of this,' she said, 'or you will end up in a mental hospital.' I did indeed end up in a mental hospital years later, but as a psychiatrist!

I knew two people who would understand about my finding Jesus in a personal way – my Uncle Glyn and Auntie Lena. Uncle Glyn, my mother's brother, was a pastor. They were different. Their faith was real and they had a joy and a solid foundation to their lives. They were always at hand to help us as a family and going to stay with them was like visiting an oasis in the desert. They were overjoyed when they received a letter from me telling of my new-found faith.

I discovered later that they had devoted a month to pray, sometimes fasting, especially seeking God for a breakthrough in our family suffering. During this time, my Aunt had 'seen' a picture in her mind's eye of our house with a light above it in the shape of a cross and was assured that God was hearing and answering their prayers. My letter arrived at the end of that month.

Only several months later did I begin to understand my need for forgiveness and how Jesus had died to obtain it for me. That made me love Him so much more and desire to spend my whole life serving him. Yet I struggled inwardly with the difference between the joy in worship and evangelism and what I was experiencing at home. I remember hours kneeling by my bed, wondering if my prayers ascended higher than the ceiling. The room felt so empty and I would think rather dramatically, 'I'm alone in the universe. There's no one who can help us.' I hid this pain in my heart for years.

I remember clearly when despair threatened to swallow me up. I was standing by the washbasin in the bathroom, when my mother switched on the radio downstairs. The next thing I heard was people singing George Matheson's amazing hymn, written in 1882.

O love that will not let me go
I rest my weary soul in thee
I give thee back the life I owe
That in thine ocean depths its flow
May richer, fuller be

It was like a message straight from heaven to my heart. That hymn would come back to me at different stages in my life just when I needed that reassurance, although there were aspects of it that would only make sense to me much later.

Chapter Three

WHERE ON EARTH HAVE I LANDED?

I did well academically and was very motivated to succeed, but didn't enjoy study. I preferred the cultural activities, especially music and drama. I was very torn about what further study to do: should I become a medical doctor because of my love of science, or go to a music and drama school to pursue a career on the stage? I loved acting – probably because I found it easier to pretend to be someone else than to be myself.

Eventually I chose medicine, but probably for all the wrong reasons: I developed a 'saviour' identity because of my family's needs – I was the caregiver, problem solver, comforter… I hated illness and wanted to try to fight against it. But the 'drama' aspect was also important because of TV programmes like Doctor Kildare and Emergency Ward 10 – the idea of running down hospital corridors with a stethoscope saving lives was very appealing.

Arriving in Leeds from a small Welsh village for my medical studies, I felt as if I had landed in New York! Being in a huge busy city with rows of traffic and high-rise buildings was so unfamiliar to me. My time there was very mixed and not without many inner struggles. It was hard to leave my needy family behind and be so far away from them. Someone remarked to me one day, 'You look as if you're carrying the weight of the world on your shoulders.' Some of my difficulties were to do with my being Welsh, something I will address in another chapter.

However, there was also much joy as I discovered so many other students with a living Christian faith. It was an exciting time when the so-called 'Charismatic renewal' was beginning to impact many churches and we were privileged to hear some great teachers who visited the Christian Union. It was wonderful to learn of and experience so much more of what the Holy Spirit could do. But underneath, there was always a sense of guilt, that I was being blessed when my family at home were suffering. In fact, it seemed that the more I was blessed and the deeper my commitment to Jesus, the harder it would be for them at home.

I remember wondering if it was really worth it. Maybe I should cool down a bit and not be so committed. But Jesus' words to His disciples, after many followers left him, haunted me: 'Will you leave me too?' I couldn't get away from Simon Peter's reply: 'Where else can we go? You have the words of eternal life.'

I soon realised medical training was not quite what I had imagined. It meant hard slog and long hours of study. I wanted to leave several times, but God wouldn't let me. I got involved with a ministry to the homeless and addicts, even moving into their hostel which was run by Christian friends. For a while I shared a room with 'street people'. They were exhilarating times as we witnessed miracles of transformation in people's lives. I was far more interested in what I considered to be 'Christian ministry' than in my medical studies. (However, I'm now convinced that every Christian is doing 'Christian work' if living for God.)

At the end of my fourth year, I was diagnosed with tuberculosis. I was feeling so exhausted and ill that being allowed to climb into bed and stay there was a huge relief. I had just come home for half term and ended up having a year out, spending 3 months in a sanatorium. That was a good experience, learning what it was like to be on the other side of the fence.

Once I had started improving and could visit other wards, I looked for people with musical talent and organised a concert for the patients who were still confined to bed. I have fond memories of those 3 months – except for injection times. One nurse gave particularly painful ones. She would call out 'Go slack everybody.' as she approached, which was the signal for us all to become very tense!

GRADUATION

Eventually I graduated and worked as a doctor in North Wales but kept asking God to 'let me out'. It was a love/hate relationship. I loved being with people and trying to help them get well, but hated the responsibility of making 'life and death' decisions under duress.

I was probably remembering all the responsibility I had to carry for my family when I was still young myself. I felt I didn't belong – a 'square peg in a round hole'. Yet I stayed in medicine for 13 years and had many precious experiences, as well as some very challenging and scary ones!

Graduation, 1972

I learnt not to 'fall apart' in the face of suffering, in order to be there for people in their times of greatest need. I really wanted to be involved in overseas mission work, but couldn't see how I could move away from my family and all their needs. So I thought I could maybe be involved with drug addicts. David Wilkerson's book 'The Cross and the Switchblade' had made a deep impression on me. It showed me how the Holy Spirit could transform hopeless lives in a truly amazing way.

During that time, I contracted meningococcal meningitis from a patient and was in a coma for five days, not expected to live. But in response to the prayers of many Christians in different parts of the world and to the surprise of the medical profession, I made a total recovery over a period of three months, in spite of serious damage to various parts of my body.

I was subsequently shown as an 'exhibit' in medical meetings and my case was described in the British Medical Journal. This confirmed my desire to live my life for God and convinced me that He could work miracles in seemingly impossible situations.

This illness happened five days after desperate prayer for my father. He was an old man of 83 years by this time and when I spoke about patients dying, I observed a 'cloud' coming over his face. He was obviously very afraid of dying and I said to God, 'I don't know how much longer he's going to live. It seems he's not ready to meet You. Please get him ready, whatever suffering that may involve.' I thought it was going to involve suffering for him not me.

In the days when I was in a coma, he suffered more than me. First he was told that, if he wanted to see me alive, he would have to come to the hospital immediately. Then, when I began to improve, he was told that if I survived, I could well have severe brain damage. After witnessing the answers to prayer as I recovered, he found a real faith for the first time. What a joy that was. I began to learn about redemption – how God could bring good out of suffering and turn loss into gain.

CONTROL

Later, when I was with Youth with a Mission (YWAM), I developed symptoms that could have indicated I was getting rheumatoid arthritis like my mother. This was very scary and I was encouraged to seek medical help. But I didn't trust doctors. On both the occasions of serious illness mentioned above, the doctors had initially misdiagnosed me, and with the meningitis this probably would have cost me my life without God's miraculous intervention.

When I refused to see a doctor, explaining my lack of trust, I was challenged that I had a problem with control. I only felt safe when I was in control of making decisions. This was compounded by growing up in a family situation which felt very out of control and unsafe. With help, I began to understand that control is a form of idolatry – trusting myself more than God. I needed to trust God that even if a doctor made a mistake, God could bring good out of it. After all, my time in the sanatorium had really been a good experience, and my dad had come to a living faith through my being healed of meningitis.

So I repented of my need to control, and renounced it. I saw a doctor, who agreed it could be rheumatoid arthritis, but thank-fully the tests were negative. After further prayer, my symptoms disappeared, but an important lesson had been learnt in the meantime. However, this need to control had been so deeply ingrained in me that it would be a lifelong learning curve.

RELUCTANT PSYCHIATRIST

A surprise phone call from a leading Psychiatrist, after his daughter heard me speak in a Christian meeting, changed the course of my life. He tried to persuade me to study psychiatry – the last thing I wanted to do. Eventually I gave in and started working in a mental hospital, where several doctors strongly encouraged me to do the full training as a psychiatrist. After a big struggle, I reluctantly agreed to do this because my pastor felt God was saying this would open doors for me in the future that wouldn't otherwise open.

So I studied and qualified as a psychiatrist. In this work I learnt many valuable lessons, especially how not to be shocked by anything. Also, to understand better why people reacted the way they did and to be able to distinguish between true mental illness and being dysfunctional, unable to cope with life's demands.

Behind closed doors in the consulting room, I had many opportunities to share my faith with patients who were open to listen, and I saw God answer some prayers in amazing ways. Some of the consultants even started to ask me for help with patients who couldn't throw off feelings of guilt, in spite of all the treatments: 'Could you try giving them a dose of your Gospel?' One consultant joked that he wished I would leave his private patients alone, because having found peace with God they didn't need his services anymore.

However I was also frustrated, with a desire to discover the root cause of people's problems, so that they could experience in-depth healing, rather than simply treating their symptoms.

We were beginning to experience in church how the Holy Spirit could heal inner wounds in ways I had never imagined. Isaiah 61:1-3 intrigued me – verses that Jesus chose to read in a synagogue in Luke 4:17-21, indicating that this is what he had come to do: *'to bind up the broken-hearted, proclaim freedom for the captives… to comfort all who mourn'…* giving them *'the oil of gladness instead of mourning and a garment of praise instead of a spirit of despair.'* Not only did my patients need that kind of healing – I did too.

I left after five years to do a much less demanding Community Medicine job, as by now I was heavily involved in pastoral church work, but couldn't wait for the day when I could leave medicine altogether.

Chapter Four

ON BEING WELSH

'Sit down!' It was my first day in school and a large lady was saying something to me that I didn't understand, until she came over and forcibly put me in my chair. These were the two first words of English for me to learn when I was four years old.

There were no Welsh-speaking schools at that time, so I had to be educated through English. It took until the Welsh Language Act of 1993 for the Welsh language to be recognised as an official language. Some of my friends were involved in non-violent protests for Welsh to be recognised as an official language – a number of them going to prison for it.

I was very aware of tension between those of us who were Welsh and the English living in Wales, who had no interest in or respect for our language and culture, never asking how to pronounce our place names properly.

There was conflict in school, especially in secondary school. I remember two girls in my class telling a Welsh friend and me, 'You're inferior to us; my father says so.'

My angry response was, 'That's not true! The problem is that you are all proud and arrogant. My father says so.'

'Why don't you just knuckle under and accept that we conquered you?'

I didn't realise at the time how deeply these words had affected me.

ON BEING WELSH

Learning, especially from my father, of many past injustices in our history which had made us feel devalued, angered me even more. 'This is what they did to us. They are all the same.'

I heard about the 'Welsh Not' – how it had been illegal for Welsh children to speak Welsh in school. Children caught speaking Welsh would have a wooden board hung around their necks and could only have it removed by reporting on a fellow pupil speaking Welsh. Whoever was wearing it at the end of the day was flogged.

My mother worked with someone whose father had refused to report any of his Welsh speaking friends, so ended up being flogged day after day. His story became famous in Wales.

We didn't learn about such injustices in school (and there were many more); instead we were taught the history of England. That meant that we learnt about the injustices in an emotive way.

There was growing resentment in my heart, 'They will never understand our pain.' Like many of my fellow-countrymen, I developed a 'wounded' identity: 'We are an oppressed people.' At the same time I had a growing concern for other people groups who felt devalued and oppressed (Aborigines, Native Americans, Maori, the Black people of South Africa…).

In secondary school all pupils were divided into five 'houses' engaging in various competitions against each other. When I was house captain, we had a competition to write and produce a history drama. I decided that I would write about Welsh history, not English history.

In fact, I would write a drama about the Welsh Not. I produced it and played the part of the schoolboy my mother had told me about, who had to wear the Welsh Not for speaking Welsh in school and was flogged day after day. The drama ended with the 'teacher' telling me that I should never speak Welsh in school again, and asking if I understood that. Trembling I was to respond, 'Yes, Miss Price.' I did so with tears and I was not acting!

RELUCTANTLY LEAVING WALES

The time came for me to apply for medical school and I wanted to study in Cardiff, the capital of Wales. I didn't get a place there but was offered one in Leeds. As you will remember from an earlier chapter, while Leeds was not my first choice of medical school, with hindsight I can see how and why God led me there. I didn't want to go to England. 'God, what are You doing to me?' I had no choice but to go, but once there I developed a sense of deep alienation.

Without my realising it, the words, 'You're inferior to us,' spoken in school came back to haunt me. I don't belong here, I thought. They are superior to me. 'What's your name? What? We can't say that. You'll have to find another name.'

I suggested Non, which is a Welsh name in itself, but they found that very amusing. Non what? Non-entity? They soon changed it to Nonny. But I didn't know who Nonny was. This increased my struggle with my identity and where I belonged. I lost all confidence and even began to develop a stammer. I thought those teaching me probably considered me stupid and unfit to be there as a Welsh person. I wanted to leave and go home.

The one thing that kept me there, was getting involved with the Christian Union. I was amazed to find so many Bible-believing Christians. There had only been a handful of us in school and we had been ridiculed. Gradually I came to trust and appreciate English friends. I also got involved with overseas student groups, feeling more 'at home' with them.

As I made friends with lovely English students in Leeds, I realised that I had judged a whole people group and Jesus takes this very seriously. Matthew 7:1-2 makes this very clear: *'Do not judge, or you too will be judged. For in the same way as you judge others, you will be judged and with the same measure you use, it will be measured to you.'*

Though outwardly being nice to everyone, inside I was harbouring bitterness and anger towards the English. I had to repent of this judgemental attitude and renounce it, as I discovered they were *not* all the same. After graduation I decided to return home to Wales and become Rhiannon again.

MORE HEALING BACK HOME

After returning to Wales, a series of events continued to change my heart. I joined a women's intercession group called Lydia, which exists in many countries. In one event, which had a profound effect on me, an English lady repented of all the innocent blood shed by the English in Wales in ancient times and I repented of all the English blood we Welsh had shed in retaliation.

A red blanket represented the shed blood and together we carried this to a cross and deposited it there. This was needed because the spilt blood still 'cries out from the ground', even if it happened generations ago.

In Genesis 4:10, God tells Cain, who had killed his brother Abel, that his brother's blood was crying out to Him from the ground. Exodus 34:7 teaches us that sin has consequences, not only in our generation, but in future generations too. This concept is also expressed in several other Bible passages, like 1 Peter 1:18-19.

In another event in South Wales, it was announced that we would deal with the sin of national idolatry. I was instantly defensive. Inwardly I was saying, 'You are the Nationalists, not us! You are the ones who imposed your language and culture on us and on other nations. All we are asking for is the right to exist. Is that wrong?'

I was the only Welsh-speaking person there and I wondered how I could leave the meeting without causing a disturbance. Then a lady stood up. She said she had specifically come from England to join us for this day and there was something she wanted to do. She crossed the room and knelt before me. She put her head on my feet and said, 'I have come here today to offer you the servant heart of an English handmaiden.'

I was puzzled, wondering what this was about. She said, 'I know you won't understand this, because in our history, you were the servants and we were the masters. Will you receive my heart today as that of a servant?'

Something inside me broke. I had never heard anyone express anything like this before and suddenly I began to feel the pain of generations of my people. Yes, I thought, this is what we have felt, like being servants to the English and I wept and wept. She kept offering me her heart. She confessed that she had only recently learnt of the injustices committed against us by the English and, weeping, began to list them. It meant so much to me that she understood our pain. I then had a choice: I could hold onto my bitterness, or I could receive her broken heart. As I saw her tears, my heart was disarmed.

I told her I would receive her heart, but that we also needed to repent, because we had hated them and resented their coming into our country. We bad-mouthed them behind their backs. We forgave each other and embraced. That day, I forgave the history of England in Wales and accepted her fully as my sister in Christ.

Note: Having forgiven the history, it is still necessary to make forgiving an on-going life-style. Many things continue to wound us, especially those of us in the Welsh-speaking community. There are still injustices and too many 'messages' that communicate the devaluing of our language and culture. Even unintentional attitudes of superiority can still reopen old wounds. Jesus' response was challenging when Peter asked how often he had to forgive. Would seven times be enough? Jesus suggested it was more like seventy times seven; in other words, he was to forgive without limit.

I still wasn't sure what to do about praying against nationalism, but I felt I could pray against nationalism becoming an *idol*, because idolatry is always wrong.

After this, I began to seek God about nationalism. Was it really wrong to love your country and want the best for her? God's answer came to me in an unexpected way. I was visiting my cousin in Birmingham and we decided to go to a concert in the town Hall because a Welsh choir was singing there. The Welsh are known for their singing and as I listened, I was so proud. I thought, this is my heritage, these are my roots. This is my true identity.

And then another thought came into my mind. I'm now convinced it was from God. The thought was: if another choir came onto this platform, made up of people who love God from every tribe and tongue, which choir would you join? The choice was not difficult - I knew that if I had to choose, I would join the international choir of believers.

So has my identity changed now that I have become a Christian, I wondered? Into my mind came the verse from 1 Peter 2:9, which says, *'You are a chosen people, a royal priesthood, a holy nation.'* I suddenly understood that God was creating a new special nation made of believers from every tribe and nation.

This was a higher identity than my natural identity, *but it still included my natural identity.* In fact, this was where my natural identity would find its healing and true purpose. The more I thought about this holy nation, the more excited I became. It's interesting that every time the word 'nation' is used in the New Testament, the Greek word is *ethne* or people group. Acts 17:26 says that *'From one man, He made every nation of men.'* God believes in people groups. They were His idea.

A CITIZEN OF THE HOLY NATION

Soon afterwards, my pastor spoke about this topic. I had never heard anyone speak about it before. He recommended a book to me by Alan Kreider, called 'Journey towards Holiness – A way of living for God's nation.' It was also based on 1 Peter 2:9 and asked interesting questions, like 'What should be the domestic policy of the Holy Nation? What about the foreign policy? What does it mean to be an ambassador of the Holy Nation?'

Since then I have studied the Scriptures further to understand more about this Holy Nation. I discovered that my new, higher identity was a wonderful one because the citizens of this nation all have equal value and can complement one another, celebrating their diversity. We are all different facets of a huge magnificent diamond, each reflecting the glory of God in a unique way. This creates something beautiful, something strong and something very valuable.

I am now much more excited about being a citizen of the Holy Nation than about being Welsh. When applying for a passport, I wish I could write 'Holy Nation' as my nationality, but then I wouldn't get a passport! But it's written on my heart.

This has changed the way I view myself in that I no longer have a 'victim' identity. But it has also changed the way I view every other people group. This has been so healing for me.

I never realised how important the 'Welsh connection' would become in my future life's work. The revelation of the Holy Nation has now become a significant key in seeking to help wounded nations find healing. In a country where there has been division, conflict or injustice, everyone's identity is wounded. Discovering a higher identity as a citizen of the Holy Nation has now given new hope to countless people.

Chapter Five

FACING MY INNER STRUGGLES

The silent retreat nearly killed me. Knowing my personality, my close friends had warned me that it could, but I was desperate. While still working as a house doctor in psychiatry and later in community medicine, I had become increasingly involved in pastoral work and counselling in the church, and it was all getting too much for me.

I had been feeling empty inside for a long time and there was an endless queue of people wanting to share their pain with me. When running on empty, one can only keep giving out for a limited time before reaching burnout. I became quite depressed and twice had to take time off work because of a duodenal ulcer. I kept trying to reduce my working hours. I was nearing the end of myself, so when someone suggested a silent retreat, I thought I'd give it a try.

The aim of that retreat was to have quality time in silence to pray and meditate, with guidance from a spiritual director in the mornings. However, after thirty minutes of silence, I had prayed about all I could think of and there were still five days to go!

During the retreat I began feeling more and more uncomfortable and stressed, and came to a painful realisation. I no longer had my actions or my words to hide behind – there was only me and God. And I was not happy. I realised that I hardly knew the God I was so busy serving and certainly didn't trust Him. By the end of the retreat I was on the verge of developing another duodenal ulcer.

I knew it was a wake-up call. It was time to remove the mask and get myself sorted out. But where should I turn for help? I remembered that I had been impressed by the teaching in a Youth with a Mission (YWAM) summer camp a few months previously and had heard them mention a Discipleship Training School. But did I need discipleship?

I had been a Christian for many years and was even teaching seminars on Inner Healing, reassuring people of how much God loved them. But evidently I didn't believe He loved *me*. The time had come to do something about it.

I left the retreat and went straight to my church elders, saying I wanted to resign from my medical job to attend a Youth with a Mission Discipleship Training School (DTS).

They were astonished and felt I didn't need to do this. I had seemed so victorious and active in ministering to others. Evidently it had been an effective mask. They tried to dissuade me, but I had been shaken by the retreat experience and knew I couldn't carry on pretending.

A few months later I enrolled at the DTS in the King's Lodge, Nuneaton, England. I asked God not to hold anything back but to face me with the truth. What was my problem? Why did I find relating to Him intimately so difficult? I wanted to find the real God – what He felt, what He thought, as I was tired of playing religious games.

The foundation of the DTS was to get to know God's character, something I had never focused on before. I well remember someone talking about fear and, being a pretty fearful person, I stood to receive prayer for various fears. Then the speaker mentioned one fear for which we needed to take time with a leader, because this would affect every aspect of our life. Whilst the reverent fear of the Lord is something very precious and necessary, there is also a *wrong* fear of God where we are actually afraid of Him and therefore keep our distance. Something registered inside me and I duly made an appointment with one of the leaders.

When I explained that I didn't really understand what my problem was, he suggested we ask the Holy Spirit for some revelation. What came to mind were the words of Jesus in Matthew 11:28: *'Come to me, all you that are weary and heavy laden.'* Yes, that was certainly me. *'...for My yoke is easy and My burden is light.'* Easy? Light? Big joke! Since when?

The leader noticed I was getting disturbed and asked what was going on for me. I exploded in anger. 'His yoke is NOT easy. His burden is NOT light.' He asked how long I had been feeling this way. I said that *nothing* had been easy.

Everyone in my family had been so needy – what was easy about that? Someone had to be strong in the situation so that had to be me. Then I had become a medical doctor and had to attend post-mortems on patients I had loved and tried in vain to help.

Then I had trained in psychiatry and tried so hard to help tormented people. One troubled young girl into whom I had sought to pour my love had gone out and committed suicide.

Now there were those endless demands for help as I was working pastorally in the church. It was all too much. It was killing me. I concluded that, far from giving me an easy yoke, God actually *enjoyed* giving me heavy ones. It seemed that around every corner there was another burden He was waiting to dump on me.

'He's just like Pharaoh,' I wept in anger. 'He's such a hard task-master! He tells me to make bricks, then increases the quota of bricks, then removes the straw and still expects me to make bricks.'

I was shocked at myself. I had never spoken like this before. I had always been a nice Christian, saying and singing all the right things. It all started to make sense. No wonder I didn't feel very comfortable close to God. Who wants to be close to a cruel Pharaoh? (You can read the story in Exodus 5.)

The leader asked me if I'd like to repent of my wrong attitudes. 'Repent?' I retorted. 'But it's true!' He concluded I wasn't quite ready to repent, but asked what I would like to say to God. 'This is where I'm at, God,' I said. 'I didn't know that all this was inside me. If I've got it wrong, please convince me. Please reveal Your *heart* to me. I've got to know the real You – what

You are thinking and what You are feeling, especially with regard to suffering humanity.'

I also committed to study God's character as revealed in the Bible.

UNFOLDING REVELATION

The next few months were like a book slowly opening for me, as I began to see God in a new light. He had not, as I had supposed, been programming horrible things on His heavenly computer to happen to my family. Most things happening on earth were not His will at all, which is why Jesus asked us to pray that His will would be done on earth as it is in heaven. Rather we were suffering the consequences of living in a cursed creation and of many sinful human choices.

I will never forget a talk given by Oliver Nyumbu from Zimbabwe, one of the course leaders, on 'The Heartbreak of the Godhead.' He opened up Genesis 6 which describes the story of Noah and the Flood, where God evaluated the effect of having given mankind the risky gift of freedom of choice. Verses 5 and 6 (NIV) tell us that seeing the extent of human wickedness, His heart was filled with pain and that He even regretted creating us. If everything about God is without limit, then His ability to feel pain is also without limit.

We use defence mechanisms to minimise the pain we feel: He doesn't. We get conditioned to things after a while: He doesn't. The greater the value of the relationship, the greater the pain when it all goes pear-shaped. We cannot begin to imagine the pain in the heart of God over the mess we have made of His beautiful creation.

I left that talk feeling rather stunned, but saying to myself, 'If this is true, it's going to change my whole outlook on life.'

I then asked God why on earth He had committed Himself to keep working with mankind, knowing how sinful we were. Why hadn't He brought it all to a halt there and then? Surely the cost of letting it continue was far too high. It would mean so much more pain for Him as well as for us and would eventually cost Him the death of Jesus. Yet, anticipating the joy of fellowship with many more people like Noah, God had decided to continue with His creation, promising not to bring the world to premature judgement, however bad it got.

I could only conclude that there must be incredible glory ahead of us. It must be that one day, when we are beyond the reach of sin and its consequences, we will look back at the whole journey, and God and man will agree that it was worth it all.

There was something I really wanted more understanding about. I had always felt dissatisfied with any simplistic explanation of the cross. I felt there had to be more.

One of our old Welsh language hymns says that even eternity will be too short to fully explore all that was happening through the shed blood of Jesus, yet it seemed we were explaining it in five minutes.

I decided to spend a day in prayer and fasting, seeking God about this. I hate fasting with a passion so this was a huge sacrifice for me. It ended up being a very disappointing and frustrating day. My mind kept wandering and as the day progressed, all I could think about was food.

No fresh revelation came, in spite of my petition, and I concluded that it had been a wasted day and I might as well have eaten. But years later, I looked back with tears in my eyes and realised that God had heard my heart's cry and had answered in an amazing way. And He is still revealing more to me today.

PUTTING IT INTO PRACTICE

During the summer holidays, I had a chance to put my new-found revelation of God's heart into practice. I decided to join a YWAM team working in the red light district of Amsterdam for a few weeks. This involved running a coffee shop called The Cleft, positioned between a Satanic temple and a pornographic show.

We also took turns to walk along the canals to try to get to know the prostitutes, seeking to share the love of Jesus with them. We discovered that these girls were hungry for real love. Some were friendly and ready to talk, but others were bitter and hard-hearted.

I remember one evening seeing an older, hard-looking prostitute the other side of the canal and sensing God wanted me to cross over to her and tell her that He loved her. She responded angrily.

'Oh yes? So where was He when my first husband was brutally beating me?' I told her that God had never wanted her to suffer in that way and that His heart was full of compassion towards her. 'So why didn't He stop it then?' she asked. Silently praying desperately for help, I suggested we took a seat and thought about what options were open to Him. What did she think He should have done?

Together we began to list the possibilities. He could have killed him; He could have paralysed him; He could have changed his thinking and taken away his desire to be so cruel. I suggested that before she chose her option, we should give God the right to do that with anyone who sinned.

She realised that with the first two options either everyone would be killed or paralysed, so with a wry grin, agreed that this was not a viable option. 'So why didn't He simply change his thinking?' she asked.

We then talked about how God had created us with an ability to freely choose for ourselves. He didn't want robots. We were created for a love relationship with Him and where there is no choice there is no love, because love is always a choice. I explained to her that God had made provision for everyone to have a new heart, a heart of love, by sending His son Jesus to die for our sins and make it possible for us to start anew. But we have to believe this and want it.

It really was quite surreal: there we were, sitting in front of a brothel, having a deeper theological discussion than happens in many churches. A client then came on the scene and she had to leave me. The next time I was in that part of the Red Light district, she saw me coming and ran to meet me, giving me a big hug. She asked if I had time to speak to the girl in the next window to hers, because she would like a similar talk with me.

Little did I think that one day I would use this experience to help those asking, 'Where was God?' to process their inner struggles in some extremely dark places. This time in Amsterdam was very significant for me. It showed me that no one is beyond the love of God. There is hope for everyone.

Chapter Six

DISCOVERING GOD AS THE REDEEMER OF EVERYTHING

Although I had learnt much about God's character on the DTS and my perspectives were changing, I was still looking for more answers, so I signed up for the next Biblical Counselling School, again with YWAM in Nuneaton.

This turned out to be not so much my learning how to counsel others, but rather God further counselling me. Remembering my years growing up, especially my teenage years, was particularly painful. When we were encouraged to look back over our lives, I could only come to one conclusion. Either God wasn't there, or He didn't care. I could find no other options. After this I sank into a deep darkness where I wasn't sure if God existed anymore.

I was struggling to hold onto my faith by my fingernails, trying to convince myself of the reasons why I was supposed to be a believer, but I lost all sense of the reality of God's presence in my life. Maybe it's easier to cope with a God who isn't there than a God who doesn't care.

In the midst of my searching for understanding, I was confronted by Luke chapter 7. Here was John the Baptist – the one who had been told by the Spirit who Jesus was and had heard the amazing confirmation direct from heaven – now sending his disciples to Jesus to ask if he really was who he was perceived to be. Jesus simply tells them to give John the evidence.

But earlier in the chapter it's clear that they had already done this. In fact, it's precisely when he hears the compelling evidence that he sends out his messengers. What sense could I make of that?

The next statement from Jesus is very telling. He says, *'Blessed is he who takes no offence in me and who is not hurt or resentful or annoyed or repelled or made to stumble whatever may occur'* (Luke 7:23 Amplified Version).

Why did He send that message back to John? What offence could John have taken at Jesus? Could it be that John was thinking, 'It's all very well you doing these wonderful things for everyone else, but you seem to have forgotten about me. The Messiah is supposed to open prison doors and set captives free, but I'm rotting here in this prison while you seem to be having a very good time.'

Meditating on this passage led to a revelation that was life-changing, namely that *taking offence at God is the seed out of which unbelief grows.*

Unbelief is not rational. It is an emotional response, rooted in being offended by God for some personal reason – some incident or season in our life where we felt abandoned by God. We then begin to think He is lying to us when He tells us that He has loved us with an everlasting love (Jeremiah 31:3).

We say inwardly, 'Don't expect me to believe that. I have too much evidence to the contrary.' I realised that I had taken offence at God because of my family's suffering and this had become an accusation in my heart against Him. My unbelief was a character assassination of God. 'You are not who You say You are!' This helped me understand the seriousness of unbelief and why it causes people to harden their hearts, like the children of Israel did and as a result died in the wilderness (Hebrews 3:15-19).

DEALING WITH THE ACCUSATIONS

At the Biblical Counselling School, we were encouraged to write a paper on a subject that was troubling us, (like rejection, lack of confidence and so on) and seek answers through studying Scripture. I became convinced that my subject had to be 'Accusation against God'.

The leaders prayed with us that it would not be an intellectual exercise but a life-changing encounter with God. Their prayers were answered. I was surprised to discover that accusation against God was a theme running right through the Bible. I particularly identified with the children of Israel in the wilderness in the book of Exodus, mounting up evidence that God was against them and their families in spite of His many gracious interventions. Their accusation was, 'When human beings are suffering, *You don't care*. When we need You, You are nowhere to be found.' I realised that this is always what we hold against God.

I heard my own voice in Naomi's bitter plea: '*Call me Marah* (which means bitterness) *because the Almighty has made my life very bitter*' (Ruth 1:20).

I understood the cynical response at the beginning of the book of Malachi when God told His people, 'I have loved you.' 'Oh really?' they seemed to be saying. 'When was that? We seem to have missed it…'

As I came to the New Testament, I saw that the accusations were gathering more and more momentum as Jesus became the focus of all mankind's accusations against God throughout history.

We are told that the Pharisees *'looked for a reason to accuse Him'* (Mark 3:2). They merely used incidents to confirm their own heart attitude of accusation.

Even His own beloved disciples echoed the sentiment of the children of Israel in the wilderness, by accusing Him in a boat in a terrifying storm of *not caring* when they were about to perish (Mark 4:38).

It would eventually culminate on Golgotha's Hill, where all the accusations of every generation were targeted at one person, because He claimed to be Emmanuel, God with us. There, mankind's fury against God would reach its climax and God would be declared guilty and worthy of death. I found myself arrested at the point where He stood in Pilate's hall and Pilate asked Him what He has to say for Himself in view of all the accusations levelled against Him (Matthew 27:13).

In the face of all these accusations, Jesus was *silent*. Why silent when He had the chance to defend Himself, I wondered. Come on, Jesus, here's Your chance! The revelation of why He was silent changed my life. *He was silent because He had come to earth to take the responsibility for everything.* Through His silence He was saying, 'I will take all your accusations and anger. Count Me guilty for everything. Put it all on Me. This is why I came.'

He knew that His answer was not to be in words, but in dying. And His dignified silence was deafening.

And there, incredibly, in the very act of taking the blame and the responsibility and submitting to all these accusations, Jesus silences them forever. I realised I had in my imagination walked up that hill carrying a pile of stones, ready to hurl at Him.

But as I looked at the cross, my heart cried out for the first time, 'NOT GUILTY! I still don't understand why we have to suffer, but I know that it's not Your fault.' In willingly making Himself totally vulnerable to my accusations, He disarmed me. When we think God *couldn't care less*, the truth is He *couldn't care more*.

That's when I began to really worship God. Up to then, my lips had been singing that He was good and loving, but my heart had not been in agreement. Now I had seen something of His heart and I really liked and trusted what I saw. There was nothing I would want to change. This was a God with whom I was truly impressed.

WASTED SUFFERING?

Finding out that God was not the author of our tragedies and especially of injustice, had been really helpful. But a few weeks later I was left with another dilemma.

Was all our suffering just a big waste, with no meaning or purpose, something that should never have happened, which had grieved the heart of God, but that He was impotent to do anything about? I couldn't live with that either.

After I had been struggling with this for some days, one of the leaders came to me at breakfast, saying that she had been lying face down, burdened to intercede for me for a couple of hours early that morning. She believed God had given her a message for me. Did it mean anything?

This was the message: 'For My children, no suffering is ever wasted, but through it I can create gold. You only see things from the viewpoint of time; I see things from the viewpoint of eternity.' It certainly did mean something. Peace settled into my troubled heart.

My greatest pain had been over my mother's suffering. I had taken up the offence on her behalf. Yet I had seen the gold. Not long before she died, when I was expressing disappointment because she had not been healed, she had said with a smile, 'No, don't be angry at God, Rhiannon. He has healed me inside, which is far more important.' If that gold was now shining in eternity, I could live with that.

That's when I began to glimpse something much bigger about God being the Redeemer. Not only has He redeemed us from a lost eternity, incredibly wonderful as that is; He has potentially redeemed *everything*.

I didn't expect to get excited reading the last chapter of Leviticus. But when I realised that everything that was redeemed (literal meaning: bought back) had one fifth added to its value (Leviticus 27:30-31), I got really excited.

On the cross, Jesus was buying back *everything* that the Thief had stolen from us. *'The Thief comes only to kill and steal and destroy: I have come that they might have life and have it to the full'* (John 10:10).

If we invite Jesus into our tragedies, He can give them back to us with added value, so that they work for our *gain*, not our *loss*. Can there be a greater victory? No wonder we read in Romans 8:37 that in Him we are more than conquerors. That had always puzzled me before. How can you be more than a conqueror? Simply being a conqueror was surely wonderful enough. But if there is nothing that God cannot redeem and we can end up in a better place whatever life throws at us, that's incredible hope for God's children. At last I understood Romans 8:28, that in everything, God is working for the good of those who love Him.

As we look at Scripture, we find that there is a wonderful pattern in all God's dealings with humanity. Although Satan robs humanity of so much of what God intended, God is able to restore us so that the final state is even better than the original one. We can think of people like Joseph, Daniel, Ruth, and others, who experienced great loss but eventually ended up on a higher level. Of course, the greatest example is Jesus Himself, who though He experienced loss to the point of crucifixion, is now exalted to the highest place and has been given a name above every name (Philippians 2:5-12).

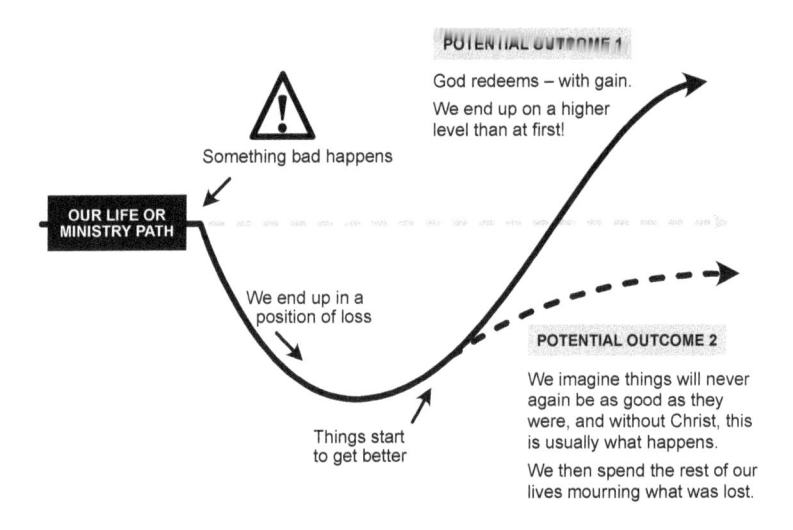

POTENTIAL OUTCOME 1
God redeems – with gain. We end up on a higher level than at first!

Something bad happens

OUR LIFE OR MINISTRY PATH

We end up in a position of loss

Things start to get better

POTENTIAL OUTCOME 2
We imagine things will never again be as good as they were, and without Christ, this is usually what happens.
We then spend the rest of our lives mourning what was lost.

This too became a key that would open for many a place of amazing healing. The experience of discovering fire lilies on a later visit to South Africa confirmed this and became a powerful symbol. So it was particularly precious to come across Kintsugi recently, the Japanese art-form of putting bits of broken pottery back together with gold in the glue: another powerful image.

OUTREACH IN MALAYSIA

At the end of my time with YWAM, I co-led an outreach team to Malaysia. We wanted to share some of the truths that had been transforming our lives with some rural churches that didn't usually receive foreign speakers.

We had a time of personal preparation before beginning our work there, and I began to meditate on the temptations of Jesus, as these had preceded His public ministry (Matthew 4:8-10). I was always puzzled by the third temptation. If it's a true temptation then the desire is very real. I'm thankful for the peers who tried to persuade me to smoke at the age of nine. I nearly choked to death. So smoking has never been a temptation. So was Jesus *really* tempted to bow down and worship Satan? Surely not!

I wondered if He was being tempted to develop the same method of working. Satan works by controlling people and has been extraordinarily successful.

So is this what Jesus was tempted to do in order to get followers? I now believe it was and He totally rejected that method. He could have walked around shining with heaven's glory, which would have caused people to fall down in wonder and fear. He could have forced people to believe in Him by taking away their freedom to choose. But instead He chose humbly to walk around incognito and allow people slowly to come to their own conclusions. The first two temptations also showed His refusal to use His divinity to manipulate people into believing. I'm so thankful now for that time of God revealing more truths to me.

It was illegal for us to share our faith with the Islamic Malays, so we worked with the Chinese and Indian communities. We discovered this was a shame / honour culture, where one never wanted to 'lose face'. This would be quite a hindrance to our being able to deal with deep heart issues, so we were on our knees asking God for His wisdom. I strongly sensed that God was saying, *'What I can use and anoint the most is your vulnerability.'*

So we took the risk and began to share our own struggles and pains, and how Jesus had helped us through them and healed our hearts. This evidently also gave them permission to risk being vulnerable, as many burst into tears and we had some very precious times of seeing God heal broken hearts.

Little did I know how important the value of being vulnerable was going to become in my future ministry. I understand now the way God really has 'ordered my steps' and that all of life's experiences can be used and shaped to become a means of blessing to other people, sometimes in circumstances that we never imagined we would encounter.

Chapter Seven

MORE EXPERIENCES OF PREPARATION

I have never been one to pray long prayers. In my early years as a believer, I had a very short prayer that I frequently prayed, taken from the story in the Gospels of the parable of the sower (Matthew 13). I would say to God, 'Not 30, not 60, I want 100% fruitfulness out of my life.'

Later as I faced various disappointments, God would remind me of my prayer and I would begin to understand that God knew the bigger picture and somehow that disappointment was going to yield greater fruitfulness in the end. In tears, I would confirm that it was still my prayer and indeed, I'm still praying it.

There were some intriguing prophetic messages given to me by Christian leaders with widely recognised prophetic gifts. One involved seeing a very high mountain range in the distance, through which he believed that God was saying that there was a work for me to do for Him which would surpass anything I had thought of or could even imagine.

Another leader said that when he looked at me he had a mental image of a harp. That's only because he knows I'm Welsh, I thought, the harp being our national instrument. But he then went on to say, '*You* are the harp and God is going to play a beautiful tune on you. But that tune is not *The Land of my Fathers* (the Welsh national anthem). It's an international tune.'

My response was, 'I have no idea how that's going to happen, so God, if this is from You, You will have to bring it about.' These words were duly stored away in the back of my mind.

In the months and years that followed, any reference to 'the nations' in Scripture or in songs would always pull at my heart. For example, Psalm 2:8 says *'Ask of me, and I will make* **the nations** *your inheritance.'* Psalm 22:27 foretells that *'All* **the nations** *and all the families of the earth will worship...'* Isaiah 49:6, 8-9 intrigued me – restoring the land, taking God's salvation to the ends of the earth and reassigning its desolate inheritances. Although written prophetically about Jesus, I couldn't help feeling that God was saying something to me through these verses and my heart would beat a little faster.

At the end of the counselling school in YWAM, we had a week's visit from Jean Darnell, a godly American Christian leader with a recognised prophetic gift. Although there had been an album prepared for visiting speakers, giving them information about each student, she had refused to look at it.

She wanted to hear directly from God without being influenced by any other source. At the end of the week, she said that she felt God had given her a message for each one of us.

Knowing one another very well by this time, we were amazed at how relevant the messages were. But when she came to me, her words were probably the most astounding, as everyone knew the struggles I had been through.

She felt that God was saying: 'Rhiannon, you have been in a dark cave, where you even doubted if I existed. I want you to know that I was not outside the cave waiting for you to come out. I was with you in the cave the whole time, even when you were not sure you believed in Me anymore. I have brought you out by the hand into the light and in future I will use you to bring many more out of darkness into light.'

I returned to YWAM after a few months to do the Basic Leadership School and heard a YWAM leader called Reona Jolie give a prophetic message to the whole group. She said that dark times of much suffering were coming to the world, when everything would be shaken. It was imperative that we were sure of our God and knew His character, as this was the only way we could keep standing firm in the midst of tribulation.

This message made a deep impression on me and getting to know God's character and helping others to know the real God became a lifelong passion. He is magnificent beyond all imagination. His humble self-giving love is mind-boggling. It is by beholding Him that we are changed (2 Corinthians 3:18).

BACK TO WALES

When I finished my invaluable training with YWAM after 18 months, I returned home to see what God had in store for me. Perhaps the biggest lesson for me on YWAM was that God is God and I am not!

During the next few years, the international aspect became more prominent in my life. Together with two friends, John and Pauline Hymus, who were leaders in Operation Mobilisation (OM), I helped to run a course in Rhyl, North Wales, for Christian workers in different parts of the world.

This was to help them deal with unhealed parts of their lives, which were hindering their mission work. We called it a Leadership School initially, as we thought that is what would attract leaders to come.

The participants were only with us for a few short weeks and would then return to remote parts of the world. We were desperate to find keys that would help them turn a corner and begin to find significant healing and transformed thinking. As we cried out to God to give us wisdom and revelation, He was so faithful. We saw many people coming to see God's character in a new light and being healed of wounds received through life tragedies.

The course highlight for me was John Hymus' teaching on 'The character of God' from Exodus 34:6-7. After Moses asks God for a revelation of His glory, God responds by revealing His character. *'And He passed in front of Moses, proclaiming, The Lord, the Lord, the compassionate and gracious God, slow to anger, abounding in love and faithfulness, maintaining love to thousands, and forgiving wickedness, rebellion and sin.'* His glory is His wonderful character.

Over the five or six weeks, John slowly took us through the original meaning of each of the characteristics listed there, studying the Hebrew roots and then seeing how this characteristic was demonstrated in the life of Jesus. It was a life-changing study. I especially loved the first characteristic God revealed, after revealing Himself as the Lord. (I'm so grateful He didn't stop there. We would have been left uncertain about Him – yes, He's Lord, but what kind of Lord is He? How is He going to treat us?)

The first characteristic is not 'The Holy One, The Judge, the One who hates sin', although all of that is true. The very first thing He wanted us to know is that He is compassionate. The root meaning of this comes from the word for a mother's womb. John was stressing that God has the same compassionate, unconditional, tender, caring love for us as a mother has for the unborn child in her womb. It can also mean 'beholding with the most tender affection' as a proud, protective father might view his newborn child – Wow!

God then goes on to say in five different ways: 'I love you, I love you, I love you…' And the last one (which some of us find difficult to understand) suggests, 'I love you so much that I take sin extremely seriously, because I know the consequence it will have, not only on you but also on your children.' This teaching was going to prove invaluable later on.

This course is still being conducted in various parts of the world under new leaders and is now called the 'Face to Face' course. It has been shortened to two weeks or so to make it more accessible. God is still using it to set many people free.

A VERY SIGNIFICANT EVENING

I will never forget one evening when I was leading a group as part of this course. We were encouraging the participants to risk being vulnerable and to share their struggles and pain in the group setting, where we would all pray for them.

One young lady shared very courageously how she had been sexually abused as a child by several men. Although now working as a missionary, she still had nightmares every night, re-living her terrible experiences and wanting to kill her abusers. She was ashamed that she had not been able to forgive and was still struggling with these thoughts. I wasn't sure how to help her and said, 'Why don't you give all this to Jesus, because He understands.' 'Oh no He doesn't,' she replied. 'How can He possibly understand what it's like to be abused as a woman?' I felt even more unable to help than before and suggested we all prayed silently, during which I desperately asked God for His wisdom.

The rather intriguing thought that came to me was this: The cross was a place of transfer, not of identification. As I thought about it this, I realised that in the Jordan River, Jesus was identifying with sinners even though He had never experienced what it was like to be a sinner.

But on the cross, something mind-blowing was happening. In 2 Corinthians 5:21 we are told that, although He had no sin, He *became* sin for us. Somehow, in a way that our limited minds can never understand, all the sin of the world was transferred to Him and He experienced the full horror of human sinfulness. (I later discovered that, '*avon*', the Hebrew word for wickedness, includes all the consequences of sin having entered the world.) So Jesus experienced on the cross not only every sin, but also every human tragedy, every pain, every injustice. It's true that in His earthly life Jesus experienced suffering of many kinds, but not all human pain and suffering. However, on the cross, He *experienced it all.*

I then tried to share with the group what God was showing me and the lady said, 'OK, I can buy that. So He does understand my pain.' I suggested that she pour it into His heart and with tears, thumping the floor with her fist, she began to do that. 'You take it all Jesus,' she said, 'I can't carry it anymore.'

The next morning, she told me that her crying the previous night had been different from every other experience of crying. Before that, she had always cried out of anger and self-pity, but that night had been a positive crying, because she knew Someone was waiting to receive it. What's more, she had slept peacefully with no nightmare.

I didn't hear from her for a few years, but then received an email saying that she had never had a nightmare again and was about to get married. Without that healing she could never have coped with getting married. I was amazed. And so thankful to God. It confirmed the truth that Jesus was not only our *sin*-bearer, He was also our *pain*-bearer. This revelation became a significant key that helped us to lead many people to a deep and lasting healing.

WORKING INTERNATIONALLY

As this work grew, we were invited to run the course in different parts of the world, which I found very exciting. I had always loved airports and flying (this has worn off by now) and I sensed that I would be travelling increasingly in God's service.

I was invited to teach on a pastoral care course on OM's ship Doulos when it was berthed in Bahrain and various people on board asked for personal counselling. After speaking and praying with an Indian lady, I suddenly remembered Britain's history in India. It was appalling. We treated them so badly. I had watched the film 'Gandhi' and was so ashamed of our history there. I remembered how much it had helped me when the English lady confessed the sins of England in Wales, and I wondered if it would help this Indian lady if I did the same.

So I hesitantly shared how ashamed and sorry I was for the way that India suffered at the hands of the British, listing some of the events I was aware of and asking her forgiveness. To my surprise she started weeping. 'I've never heard anyone from Britain say anything like this before,' she said. 'Thank you so much! I can't tell you how much this means to me.'

She then took off a beautiful necklace she was wearing and put it on my neck. 'Wear this and know that an Indian has forgiven the British,' she said. That day I learnt how powerful it is when someone confesses the sins of their nation to bring healing to the wounded heart. This also would become a significant key in the future.

GOING DEEPER

I have always been hungry for more understanding. I never want to stop seeking. I'm so aware that we only see in part and that there's so much MORE. I also made a commitment

MORE EXPERIENCES OF PREPARATION

to share with others whatever revelation God gives me. Acts 3:6 became very meaningful to me. Peter said to a crippled beggar, *'Silver or gold I do not have, but what I have I give to you. In the name of Jesus Christ of Nazareth, walk.'* We can't give what we don't have. I realised I had to really believe what I taught to be able to give an authentic message, or my words would have a hollow ring to them.

One day I read Genesis 15:5, where God takes Abraham outside at night and says, *'Look up at the heavens and count the stars – if indeed you can count them. So shall your offspring be.'* I sensed God was saying to me, 'Take a walk with Me under the stars. You will also have many descendants, more than you can number.'

It made no sense to me at the time, but I never forgot it. Isaiah 54:13 also seemed to grab my attention. *'All your sons will be taught by the Lord, and great will be your children's peace.'* (Literally: their shalom, wholeness.) I still wasn't married, to my disappointment, so how could this be true? Once when bemoaning my unmarried state, I began to sense that God was saying He had something better for me, but I reacted against it, 'No, I don't want anything better.' By now, the whole of Isaiah 54 is incredibly precious to me.

Although I had received a lot of healing while with YWAM, I still struggled at times with a need to justify my existence.

One day, I noticed a poster of the ancient poetic writing *Desiderata* by Max Ehrmann. The line, 'You are a child of the universe… You have a right to be here' leapt out at me and I embraced it. That made a huge difference later when having to make trips to London to visit foreign embassies in search of visas. God can use anything for our healing.

I also struggled to know how to pray for tragic happenings that I saw on the TV news. Where was God in all this? How could He allow innocent people to suffer in this way?

I remember being particularly grieved during the trouble in the Tiananmen Square protest (Beijing 1989), watching courageous students seeking democracy and standing still before tanks that were rolling towards them. I heard that their protest was forcibly put down and many were massacred. How on earth should one pray about a situation like that?

When I asked God about it, a verse from the second chapter of the book of Hosea came to mind. God says He will turn the valley of Achor (meaning trouble) into a door of hope. Yes, they have lost their hope, I thought. They trusted that their protest would lead to political changes and now that hope had been crushed. This is their chance to discover the true hope, which is only found in Jesus.

Whenever I heard the name Tiananmen Square or thought of it again, I would pray another one-line prayer. 'Lord, make the valley of Achor a door of hope.'

I was overjoyed when, several years later, I happened to notice a brief news item in a Christian magazine stating that several of the students who had led the Tiananmen Square protest were now believers. That taught me something very important. There is always something that God can do. 'Lord, please redeem this,' is a prayer that can be prayed with faith about any disaster.

MY PASSION

I have always loved Handel's oratorio '*The Messiah*'. I remember as a young believer listening to it all the way through, lying on the floor of the lounge. The choral piece '*Surely, surely, He has borne our griefs and carried our sorrows*' was particularly moving for me, though at that time I didn't really understand it. I was so moved by the whole music that I was determined to find all the Scriptures mentioned and was so happy when I finally managed to locate each one in the Bible.

Isaiah 53 became a very significant chapter for me, as I came to understand that it was a prophetic passage foretelling Messiah Jesus' suffering on the cross. Verse 11 states that He will see the result or fruit of His anguish and be satisfied. That became my passion. I later learnt that the prayer and motivation of the Moravians was 'that the Lamb who was slain would receive the reward of His suffering.' That touched me deeply, because this is what was in my heart too. My greatest desire was that Jesus would see what was happening in people's hearts – people being healed, restored, and transformed – and say, 'for this it was worth it all.'

For some time I had a growing desire that Jesus would be able to return to a Bride (His church) who is whole and beautiful, not one who has fractures and open wounds. I wanted God's people to be able to see the beauty in each other and celebrate their diversity instead of seeing it as a threat. Little did I know that life was going to take an unexpected turn, so that I could start seeing some of these passions become a reality.

Chapter Eight

LESSONS LEARNT IN LIBERIA

The invitation to Liberia came as a total surprise. I had phoned Youth with a Mission (YWAM) in Harpenden asking if they needed me on a team in Romania and they said, 'The place they really need you is Liberia.' I said, 'Wait a minute – where is Liberia?' Hearing it was in West Africa, I said, 'Well, I have no plans to go to Africa. Anyway why do they need me there?' Hearing there was a Civil War there, I said, 'Well, I *definitely* have no plans to go anywhere where there's a Civil War!'

I thought that was the end of the matter, but they kept phoning me. They said an international Christian relief organisation called Medair were holding a programme there working with war victims and they thought that my medical and psychiatric training would be just what they needed on that team.

For three months I struggled with this, especially when a friend asked me did I think it was really fair to my sister, who has learning disabilities and is my only close sibling, to go and put myself in danger. Eventually I came to the conclusion that God loved her a lot more than I did and He would only let me be killed if it was going to work in her best interest.

I had a tearful time of prayer, handing over my sister into God's hands and especially dealing with my guilt regarding her. Then I very hesitantly agreed to go and immediately there was peace in my heart. I even thought I might not be coming home and amazingly God helped me to be willing to lay down my life for the Liberians if that was needed.

I'm so glad I went to Liberia! While there I fell in love with Africa, learnt so much and experienced God's amazing grace in the middle of Civil War. I saw the beauty of God's people who, in spite of incredible suffering, were still able to joyfully praise and trust God. I realised that these people have so much to teach us Europeans. Some of those experiences would prove very significant in my future ministry.

FAITH OR PRESUMPTION?

One important lesson learnt in Liberia was the difference between faith and presumption. I had walked under a hot sun to visit an old lady in a very poor dwelling. Seeing me arrive all sweaty, she immediately fetched me some water in a tin mug. I had no idea how clean that water was and had to make an instant decision. Knowing it would be hurtful to reject her kind offer, I quickly prayed asking God to disinfect the water and drank it with no bad effect.

A little later I was at some meeting where they were serving 'Koolaid', a drink made by stirring coloured flavoured powder into water. I was thirsty and thought, 'Oh I'm sure I'll be fine,' and drank it. I was *not* fine. I was really sick for several days. During that time the team came into my room in the middle of the night telling me to quickly get up and hide because we were having an armed robbery. I remember murmuring groggily, 'I don't care what they steal as long as they leave the toilet.'

THE STADIUM BOYS

When I arrived in Liberia in February 1992, the capital city, Monrovia, had been liberated and was under the protection of an African peacekeeping corps but the rest of the country was still in rebel hands.

During the Civil War many young people had been forcibly conscripted into the rebel army by their leader Charles Taylor and drugged to make them commit atrocities.

Between 5,000 and 15,000 boys and girls, some as young as eight or nine years, had been coerced into joining the army in fear for their lives and taught to use modern automatic weapons. Under the influence of alcohol and drugs, they killed many.

While we were there, the government transmitted a radio broadcast encouraging any young people who did not want to kill their fellow Liberians to defect from the rebel camp and return to Monrovia.

They promised that these young people would be granted amnesty and rehabilitation. Hundreds defected. Sadly some of them were killed as they tried to escape. The young ones who made it to the capital were put into special homes, but the older ones were housed in a sports stadium on the outskirts of the city not far from enemy lines. The population feared them because these young people had all killed.

The government officials approached us as a Christian relief organization, asking if we could help them to find a new heart, because without a change of heart no rehabilitation programme would be effective. The team immediately looked at me saying this was my 'thing'. My own heart leapt and I felt I would love to be involved with these boys.

I arranged to meet with the programme leaders at the stadium to discuss what they would like from me as a Christian. I'll never forget that first day. When I arrived I saw everything was in uproar and the director sitting at his desk with his head in his hands. He said there had been a riot, the boys had been very destructive and they didn't know what to do. He said there was no point talking that day. I said, 'Maybe today is the best day to talk.'

So he called his staff and asked them to round up the boys – about 120 of them altogether – and gather them in a large room that was part of the stadium complex.

Then to my horror he said to the staff, 'OK, we all need to go out and leave this woman with them.' I was aghast, thinking, 'Oh my goodness! I haven't planned for this or prepared anything. What on earth do I do?' So I prayed fervently to God for help and then asked Him, 'When You look at these faces what do You feel?' The word that immediately came into my mind was 'excited'.

So I said to the boys, 'I've just been asking God what He feels about you and He told me that He's excited. That's because He knows that some of you are going to come to know Him and be changed people and some of you will be godly leaders in the future Liberia.' I told them that God looks at us according to what we're going to become, not according to what we are at the moment. He is a God of hope who believes in us. They were so shocked!

They started coming up to the front to shake my hand, calling out 'Will you come here and teach us the word of God?' I said that I would love to, and that began a very exciting time of meeting three times a week with these young people and helping them to get to know God's ways. (I wasn't the only one going in. Some local psychologists and evangelists also went in and a number of the boys became believers.)

We had some wonderful times together. One of my favourite memories is their dancing round the room singing, 'Jesus power – super, super power; Satan power – less, less power'. Of all the sessions I led, the one that had the most impact was a session on knowing God as a Loving Father.

KNOWING GOD AS A LOVING FATHER

As I listened to how fathers spoke to their children in the streets, I noticed that fathering could be quite harsh in that culture and wondered what effect that had on these boys as they grew up. Did they accept that as normal in their culture, or was there an ache in their heart for something different? I knew that no rehabilitation programme could transform them if they didn't know God as a loving Father. That had been life-changing for me.

The leader of the Medair team had come with me that day and told his own story of not receiving love from his father, but then discovering God as a good Heavenly Father. So I said to them, 'Today we're going to design a perfect father.' Behind me was a big blackboard the whole length of the wall. I asked them to tell me the characteristics of a perfect father. They couldn't think of anything. Then one hesitantly said, 'I think a perfect father wouldn't beat you too terribly.' I agreed and then they mentioned other negative things a perfect father would not do. I suggested we should look at some positive things that a perfect father would do, but they still couldn't think of anything.

I said, 'Let me make a suggestion. A perfect father would care if we were hurt and upset inside and would want to comfort us.' 'That's a good one!' they said. 'Write that down.' So I wrote that on the blackboard.

They then started to get the idea and we had a most amazing time as they began to imagine how a perfect father would behave. Soon the blackboard was filled with characteristics and they got really excited about the concept of a perfect father. I then told them that those who had put their trust in Jesus already had this perfect Father.

We told them there were verses in the Bible that mentioned all of these characteristics in describing Father God. He was the perfect Father we were all looking for. They asked, 'Where does it say that in the Bible? Show us.' There were only two or three Bibles between the whole group, so they began to crowd around those who had one.

I silently prayed for help, asking God to remind me where I could find the relevant Scriptures. My allocated time with them was up, but they didn't want to leave. They were so eager to find proof that the Heavenly Father really was this good, so we took about another hour finding the Scriptures.

At the end of that time a young man standing at the back said, 'I'm no Christian. I'm Muslim but I don't see no father of love like this in my religion. I want this Father of love!'

The boys who had already become believers through the visits of other Liberian pastors ran towards him and all started praying for him at the same time. It was chaotic, but so wonderful and I was amazed. It showed me that, whatever our culture, whatever our beliefs, we all need this perfect Father. We were designed by God to need this kind of father and only He could meet that need. Years later, this would become a key teaching in our reconciliation workshops. The most healing place for us is in the embrace of our loving Heavenly Father. However there was another session that became very significant as well.

GOD'S HOLY TRIBE

During another visit to these boys, I shared my story of growing up in Wales, feeling very hurt because of the injustices committed against my tribe. I told them how God had healed my heart as I forgave the tribe who had wounded us, but also by helping me find a new, higher identity. I showed them the verse from 1 Peter 2:9: *'You are a chosen people, a royal priesthood, a holy nation'* and how I had realised that out of every believer in every nation, God was forming a new special tribe.

The citizens of this Holy Tribe all speak their different languages and have their own cultures, but would celebrate diversity and love each other as equals. I told them how I had become much more excited about being a citizen of the Holy Tribe than about being a member of my own tribe.

One of the boys stood up and said, 'If we join God's Holy Tribe, then we don't need to kill each other no more!'

That's an amazing insight, I thought. That can really make a difference in these boys' lives in future. Later, as God led me into a ministry of ethnic reconciliation, the concept of the Holy Nation would become a foundation of our workshop.

MINISTERING TO REFUGEES

As the conflict continued in many parts of the country, displaced people began to pour into Monrovia. Our Medair team offered to help these fleeing refugees in whatever way they could – picking up the weak and straggling in our vehicles and ferrying them to safe shelters.

I offered to meet the survivors to help them process their losses and a meeting was arranged. Tears come to my eyes as I recall that meeting. Many had horrendous stories to tell. Especially heartbreaking were tales of families fleeing for their lives, having to leave behind the infirm and elderly to die or be killed.

These memories tormented them – how could they have failed their loved ones at their time of greatest need? I was asking God how I could help them and sensed He was encouraging me to tell my own story, describing the events surrounding my mother's death many years previously. It would be the first time I had done this publicly.

Not long after I qualified as a doctor, my mother, who was very precious to me, suffered a stroke and my sister, who has learning disabilities, was very distressed and agitated. I had to go to attend to my sister's needs but while I was with her, my mother lost consciousness and died not long afterwards. I could not forgive myself for not being with her in her hour of greatest need. For years this tormented me and I would often weep myself to sleep. However everything changed for me when God revealed to me that my mother had not been alone. She was His precious child and Jesus had been with her. He had never abandoned her. This brought me so much comfort.

I hesitantly shared that story with them and many started to weep, saying, 'Thank you Jesus! Thank you Jesus!' The whole meeting ended very positively and they were so grateful for the help they had received. I will never forget the song that they sang from their hearts with those wonderful African harmonies and tears running down their faces. It was the first time I had heard the song by Jimmy Swaggart:

> *Let Your living water flow over my soul*
> *Let Your Holy Spirit come and take control*
> *Of every situation that has troubled my mind*
> *All my cares and burdens onto You I roll*

Later, in post-genocide Rwanda, I met many who had been unable to be present when their loved ones died during the genocide, as people were fleeing in panic in all directions, or because they lived in different parts of the country. So often this adds to the trauma in other situations, such as the Covid pandemic. Because I had experienced the positive response when I shared my story in Liberia, I decided to do so in Rwanda too and it brought comfort to so many, though always at an emotional cost to me.

A MUSTARD SEED THAT WOULD GROW INTO A TREE

Our Medair team was approached by a representative of the United Nations High Commission for Refugees (UNHCR) to see if we would participate in a series of trauma-healing lectures. My name was put forward. I spoke to the organiser and explained that my teaching was all from a biblical basis. She said that would be no problem; the Muslims could also speak from their perspective.

I then heard that they were organising what they called a 'Laboratory Day' to help heal their own wounds before running this course. I was very interested to know how they would conduct it and asked if I could participate. At the beginning of the day the organiser stressed that this was to be a non-religious day. I wondered how they were going to be healed in one day's meeting together.

During the day they conducted an interesting exercise. They were asked to write down five bad things they had seen being done to someone else, five bad things they had experienced themselves and five good things that were happening in the midst of it all.

During the feedback time we heard some terrible stories and I wondered how they were going to deal with these. I particularly remember someone reading a poem he had written about Fendel University, Monrovia, where there had been a big massacre. It was a very poignant, satirical poem, with phrases like: 'Come and enrol in Fendel University. Learn how to study man's inhumanity towards man! Learn how to kill your fellow man!' I remember the whole group dissolving into tears and there was a long silence.

Then someone started to sing Joseph Scriven's hymn, *'What a friend we have in Jesus'*, and the whole group rose to their feet, holding hands with arms lifted high. For the next 30 minutes or so, they sang one hymn after another. The second was, *'On Christ the solid rock I stand; all other ground is sinking sand'* by Edward Mote.

When the singing stopped, a man called Amos stood up and said, 'I know this is a non-religious day, but it's only Jesus who has healed my wounds.' The organiser confessed that she didn't know any other way to heal wounds either and turned to me as the only person who had not gone through the Liberian Civil War. She asked if I would pray for them and ask Jesus to heal their wounds. Of course I was very happy to do that.

Years later, in post-genocide Rwanda, I remembered this exercise and it became the foundation of an activity centred around the cross, which by now has been the means of healing millions of people in different parts of the world.

Something was birthed in my heart in Liberia. I had worked as a medical doctor, dealing with bodies in pain; then as a psychiatrist, dealing with minds in pain; then as a Christian counsellor, dealing with hearts in pain.

Now I had experienced God dealing with nations in pain and I knew I could never be the same again. I didn't know if I would ever have such an experience again, but I wanted to know more about God healing nations. I had learnt valuable lessons there in Africa and was eager to know if they could be applied in other nations experiencing conflict and pain.

The psychologists who had been on our team had written a report on the work we had been involved in, which was called the psycho-social project. This had been a trial run as part of Medair's relief work and was becoming popular among relief organisations. To my surprise and disappointment, they concluded that there was no place for a Biblical approach to inner healing in such a project; it should run only on the basis of a secular psychological understanding. With a sinking heart, I therefore thought, 'Maybe that's the end of my kind of involvement.'

My first visit to Liberia lasted six weeks. My second, later that year, was for eight weeks and at the end of it I was bitterly regretting that I hadn't planned to stay longer.

People were so responsive and there was so much still to do. I was frustrated that my attempt to change my ticket had failed, even though I had a 'flexible' ticket and I wondered why God didn't help me to get it changed.

As the plane took off and I looked down on the capital, Monrovia, I was both angry and sad: angry with God and in tears at having to leave. There were people I loved down there. Why couldn't I have stayed longer? Would I ever return?

Arriving home the next day, I heard the news that at 2 am, Charles Taylor's rebel army had bombed Monrovia killing 3,000 people. Our relief team had managed to get out just before the rebels took over the airport.

On the one hand I was heartbroken. Were any of the people I loved among the casualties? What about the stadium boys – had they been recaptured? Killed? On the other hand, I felt, 'Oh Rhiannon! God knew what He was doing when you couldn't change your ticket. Why didn't you trust Him?' I'd like to be able to say that I learnt my lesson and have since always trusted God's timing when things didn't go as I thought they should, but I'm afraid I'm a slow learner. To this day, I don't know what happened to any of my contacts there.

Chapter Nine

INVITATION TO RWANDA

As with Liberia, the invitation to Rwanda came as a total surprise. In September 1994, I received a phone call from the leader of Medair, speaking from Rwanda. 'Have you been watching the news?' he asked. 'There has been a terrible genocide against the Tutsi here. We are here doing humanitarian work, giving out food and medicines and burying bodies. But in the churches, the pastors are asking if forgiveness and reconciliation will ever be possible in a situation like this. I know that in Liberia you worked quite a lot with the churches. Can you come and do the same here?'

I had seen the news and had felt horror at what I had seen, but had never considered going there. 'Don't you remember the psychologists' report?' I responded. 'They felt that only a secular psychological approach was valid.' 'I don't want a psychologist here,' he said. 'I want you.'

I protested that life was very busy. I was fully occupied running courses for missionaries and I only had two weeks free in a fortnight's time and no other 'gaps' in my timetable till the end of the year. 'Please come for those two weeks,' he said. I held the phone in my hand, trying to think of a good reason to say how impossible that would be. But he was very insistent and I remembered what a blessing the experience in Liberia had been. Why not? I thought. So on the spur of the moment, I agreed.

Over the next two weeks I began to read about what had happened in Rwanda and the more I read, the more horrified I became. The situation there was even worse than it had been in Liberia. Up to a million people had been killed in 100 days.

The whole country was in huge trauma and many had fled to the surrounding countries. I began to panic. What on earth could anyone do in a situation like that, let alone one little woman from Wales? Why had I been so foolish as to accept this invitation? At that time, Rwanda was the most wounded nation on earth!

The night before leaving, I had not packed my bag and was in total panic. In a few hours, I thought, I will get off a plane and someone will expect me to do something and I have no idea where I will even begin. How can I possibly go?

The doorbell rang and a friend stood there. 'I was just praying for you,' she said, 'and the Holy Spirit impressed on me that I should come round and remind you of the story of the feeding of the 5,000' (Luke 9:10-17).

God spoke to me through that. I felt He was saying, 'Rhiannon, I am still God and I still know how to multiply insignificant offerings.' I broke down and said, 'OK God, I'll go. If You can multiply my few loaves and fishes, I'll trust You.' And that is the only reason I went. My fear had not been of going into the situation, but of having nothing to offer.

As I flew into Rwanda for the first time and looked down on this beautiful country, wondering what could possibly heal the wounds, I felt God saying that there was only one thing powerful enough and that was the cross of His Son.

So I knew that, somehow, people had to come together at the foot of the cross. I did not know then that Rwanda had been a land of revivals and that one of the key sayings during a revival was, '*The ground is level at the cross,*' meaning that we all approach the cross on the same basis. It was clear that the cross would have to be central in all that was to be done.

WHAT LED TO THIS GENOCIDE AGAINST THE TUTSI?

The atrocious killings were the climax of efforts by one group to exterminate the other. The cause can be traced back many years:

• Until 1959 the Tutsi were in power and the Hutu (and many grass-roots Tutsi) suffered various injustices.

• In 1959 the Hutu overthrew the Tutsi monarchy in a bloody revolution that killed many and forced thousands into exile.

• The Tutsi remaining in Rwanda were discriminated against and there were several waves of massacres in the following years, with no one brought to justice.

• Three decades later, the exiled Tutsi attempted to return home and, in an effort to stop them, the Hutu government, who refused the idea of power sharing, planned the 'final solution', which consisted of exterminating all Tutsi.

• In 100 days, around one million Tutsi were brutally slaughtered. Moderate Hutu who opposed the killings were also killed in the process.

THE ROLE OF THE COLONIALISTS

Rwanda was a fairly peaceful country before the colonial era. Although some believe that the Tutsi originally came from a Nilotic group, many now believe the groupings of Hutu and Tutsi were more social groups than ethnic ones. The first European country to colonise Rwanda was Germany. After the First World War, Belgium took it over. Both countries formalised the groupings and used the 'divide and rule' policy to favour one group against the other, in order to stay in power. This led to years of conflict and injustice. The colonial role will be expounded a little more in chapter 14.

EXPERIENCING THE AFTERMATH OF THE HORROR

The smell of death was everywhere. Just 12 weeks after the genocide against the Tutsi had been brought to an end, I was based in Nyamata, one of the places that had experienced the greatest number of killings.

Churches were blood-stained, some still containing the unburied bodies of victims. I looked into the empty eyes of a greatly diminished population that had lost hope.

We drove through empty villages, whose inhabitants were either dead or had fled. Orphans pined for lost parents; parents pined for lost children. But mostly it seemed people were numb – in a state of shock. 'How could this have happened? How could he/she have done this? And he was an elder in the church!' I encountered fear, pain, anger, disbelief, but most of all, hopelessness.

I cried out to God, 'Do You have hope for this situation? If not, I may as well go home. I have to know what You feel.' As I sought God's answer, I was reminded of a verse: *'May the God of hope fill you with all joy and peace as you trust in Him, so that you may overflow with hope by the power of the Holy Spirit'* (Romans 15:13). The God of hope? I realised that this is His name – He cannot be otherwise. Wherever He is, there is hope, even in a country that has just gone through genocide.

I asked Him about the source of His hope and three things came to mind. God's hope was primarily in the finished work of His Son on the cross. Jesus had already done all that was necessary to heal Rwanda. What we had to do was to appropriate what He had done. The second was that God had not withdrawn His Spirit in spite of all the evil that had taken place. I remembered Keith and Melody Green's lovely song '*There is a Redeemer*,' which says in the chorus:

> *Thank You, Oh my Father*
> *For giving us Your Son*
> *And leaving Your Spirit till*
> *The work on earth is done*

The third point was that His hope was in His people – but the church was implicated in the genocide.

WHERE WAS THE CHURCH?

Although there were heroes of faith who did not agree with the genocide and risked their lives to save their neighbours, the tragic fact is that no church leader had publicly opposed the genocide by stating that this was a heinous sin against God and had to stop.

In the face of such horror, not only had the church been silent, but many church members and church leaders had participated in the killings. It seems some top leaders had even been implicated in planning it.

In a country where more than 80% of the population claimed to be Christian and attended a Christian church every Sunday, something must have been very wrong with what was being preached from many pulpits for a genocide involving a large part of the population to take place.

Surely the best way to prevent another genocide was to target those who, Sunday by Sunday, had the ear of most of the population. It was clear in my mind that the healing work had to start within the church. A wounded church could not be used to heal anyone.

SIGNS OF HOPE

During that first visit I had the privilege of attending some of the first Sunday services being held after the genocide. Congregations were coming together and finding out who was still around – who had been killed and who had fled the country.

What I found so moving was the praise and worship that I experienced. One choir, which had once numbered over a hundred members, now had only 12, but they still sang and praised God with such passion. There were action songs – something that is very cultural there. I remember one that showed the believer's welcome to heaven. Two by two, they played Jesus embracing the believer and wiping away the tears, showing him/her all the glories of heaven. I also remember one church group singing their translation of George Duffield's hymn, *'Stand up, stand up for Jesus.'* I thought of the poignancy of the second verse in their context and it brought tears to my eyes:

> *Stand up, stand up for Jesus, The fight will not be long*
> *Today the sound of battle, The next the victor's song*
> *To him that overcometh, The crown of life will be*
> *Who with the King of Glory, Will reign eternally*

I visited an orphanage and heard the sound of singing coming from one room. When I asked about it, they said, 'Oh – they're the Christians.' When I entered the room, I discovered a group of orphans singing from their hymn book, songs about heaven. This was their comfort – remembering that their parents and loved ones were now safe in heaven.

I was also very moved to hear many tell me that in spite of the terrible genocide, their favourite Scripture was 2 Corinthians 4:17-18: *'Our light and momentary troubles-are achieving for us an eternal glory that far outweighs them all. So we fix our eyes not on what is seen, but on what is unseen. For what is seen is temporary, but what is unseen is eternal.'*

This was all so heart-wrenching and challenging, but I noticed that all their focus was on heaven. It was the only place where they could have any hope and I realised that was something that needed to change. God also gives us hope for this hurting world now.

Chapter Ten

MEETING CHRISTIAN LEADERS IN KIGALI

I was speaking about the pain of bereavement, yet they were smiling, even laughing and there were frequent cries of 'Hallelujah' and 'Imana Ishimwe' (Praise God). I was astounded. How could they be full of praise? Didn't they have questions about where God was in all this? It was only 12 short weeks since the genocide against the Tutsi had been brought to an end and it had been arranged that I would meet a group of Christian leaders from different denominations in the capital, Kigali, to begin to explore how God could heal their very wounded hearts.

During the morning break, I went over to Antoine Rutayisire, the then leader of African Evangelistic Enterprise. I had just discovered that he had been further educated at the University of Bangor, my hometown and knew some of my Christian friends there. 'How do you express grief in your culture?' I asked. 'We don't,' he responded. 'In Rwanda, there is a widely held belief that talking about things that have wounded us and showing emotion is a bad thing which makes matters worse. Such views are reinforced by proverbial sayings such as: 'A man's tears should flow into his stomach;' 'What a man hides in his heart a dog cannot steal.'

He said that from toddlers they were taught to be strong and hide their emotions. If someone hurt them they should laugh, not cry, otherwise their enemy could take advantage of their weakness at a later date. Never making oneself vulnerable and being tough in all circumstances was a highly prized cultural value. This explained what to me had seemed a strange and inappropriate reaction to my speaking about the pain of their bereavement.

I had come to try to help them with their trauma, but if they weren't allowed to talk or express emotion, what on earth was I going to do? Was there any way to overcome this? I quickly prayed for wisdom and decided I should describe some of the features of our own British culture to the group, such as the 'stiff upper lip' and our unwillingness to 'wear our hearts on our sleeves'. 'We like to appear strong and in control,' I explained. 'We don't want to be seen expressing weakness.' 'We understand you,' they said. 'We are just like you.' I asked them if it was the same in the neighbouring countries of DR Congo and Uganda. 'Oh no,' they replied. 'They cry. Loudly.'

'So how are we to evaluate our different cultural beliefs about this?' I asked. 'How can we know which approach is most helpful to our healing?' Some suggested asking the medical people, but others said, 'No, their approach is Western. We are different.' 'How about looking in the Word of God?' someone else suggested. We agreed that the Bible is on a higher level than all our cultures and we can all learn from it.

They set about doing a quick Bible study in small groups to find out whether the Bible agreed with Rwandan and British cultural beliefs with respect to the expression of emotion.

The groups all reported the same conclusion: that the Bible does not support Rwandan and British beliefs. 'The characters in the Bible were not afraid to weep publicly,' they said. 'Even the *men*. Abraham wept as he buried Sara; King David wept publicly when Absalom died; even Jesus Himself wept at Lazarus' tomb.' They concluded that if it was OK for Jesus to show emotion, to be transparent about what was in His heart, maybe it could be so for them too.

THE GIFT OF VULNERABILITY

So this culture applauds wearing a mask, I thought. Isn't this what I also did for many years? But we needed to go deeper than mere cultural differences. It's not easy to admit that you are having doubts about God's love and questioning His goodness. I too had struggled with doubts about God's character. Outwardly I had smiled and was seemingly a victorious Christian, but inside I had been screaming in pain.

I remembered my experience in Malaysia (see end of chapter 6), another culture where no one must ever lose face. God had impressed on us that what He could use most effectively was our vulnerability and this is what gave them permission to remove their masks. Was that going to be true here in Rwanda too? However, what I had suffered was nothing compared to their terrible suffering. Yet God impressed on my spirit that this was what I should do.

I began to tell them my story. I described my sister's brain damage and suffering and then my mother's cruel disease and suffering and how it affected us as a family.

I explained that when I was 16 years old, I asked Jesus to be my Saviour and was filled with joy when worshipping at church or when involved in evangelistic outreaches. But then I had to go home and it seemed that God did not cross the threshold with me. I couldn't find any evidence of His love intervening there. I prayed and prayed, but instead of getting better, things only got worse.

I wondered if my prayers ever got higher than the ceiling. I felt so alone, trying to be the burden-bearer for my family. I concluded that if God was love, He certainly didn't love us. In fact, it seemed He was against us. Were we under a curse or something? How could a loving God allow my family to suffer so much?

I described the quandary I was in when I sensed that other believers expected me to be victorious. My solution was to wear a nice mask. When asked how I was, I replied, 'Fine', and I smiled and praised the Lord.

Yet my heart was in turmoil. Was I going to lose my faith? The thought scared me: if I lost my faith, there would be no hope for my life. So I tried to push my doubts away, swallow my pain and be the good Christian I was expected to be. It seemed to me that the church rewarded denial.

As I was relating my story, all over the room I could hear the 'Eh' and 'Tt' sounds that Rwandans make when their hearts are touched. From their faces I could see that they were identifying with me. There were some sombre nods as I expressed my questions. I explained to them that many godly people in the Bible had also struggled with such questions during times of great trial. I urged them not to be afraid of admitting their struggles. God would not condemn them. He understood their pain and was actually suffering with them. I told them my own experience – that only when I eventually took off the mask and expressed my pain and anger could God reveal Himself to me in a much deeper way and heal my wounded heart.

EARLY RESPONSE…

It's very hard for Christian leaders to acknowledge their doubts and struggles in public, especially when meeting with other church leaders. I asked them what the people walking the dusty paths of Rwanda were saying about God in the light of the genocide:

'They are saying that God abandoned us,' they said. 'We have a saying that wherever God goes during the day, He always comes back to sleep in Rwanda. Now He doesn't even do that…'

'We must be the worst people on earth for God to punish us this way…'

'God is impotent and Satan is stronger than Him…'

'They even killed God in the genocide…'

'God must be cruel and on the side of the Interahamwe (the militia who carried out the genocide against the Tutsi)…'

Eventually someone said,

'It's not only people outside. Even us, the Christian leaders, are also struggling with these thoughts.'

'Thank You, Lord,' I silently prayed. 'Now that the masks are coming off, we can get somewhere.' I suggested to them that the most important thing for us to do in order to find healing was to acknowledge the questions in our hearts and search together for answers. I put forward four questions which people might be thinking and asked if they would like to consider them:

• Is God just? If so, why is there so much injustice in the world?

• Is everything that happens in the world the will of God?

• If God is all-powerful, why doesn't He stop people from doing evil things?

• If God is all-loving, why does He let innocent people suffer?

They agreed that these questions were very relevant to their situation and they would like to seek the answers. So they got into small discussion groups and for the next hour or so they shared ideas. The feedback time was very lively and sometimes a bit heated, especially about whether or not everything was God's will. We explored the interface between God's sovereignty and man's free choice. Clearly we were going to have to address this issue before we could expect any significant healing to take place.

THE WELSH CONNECTION

I had never imagined that being Welsh would turn out to be so significant. I was frustrated to discover that we were not allowed to talk about the different groups. 'There are no Hutu and Tutsi in Rwanda anymore,' they said. 'We are all Rwandans and there are no such things as tribes here. That was a colonial invention.'

To look back at history to try to discover the roots of the terrible genocide against the Tutsi was definitely not politically correct. I wondered how I could give them any meaningful help if I was not permitted to address these issues. I had read various interpretations of their history, which seemed to depend on who was writing it. I suddenly had an inspiration. 'I grew up in one tribe hating another one,' I said. They were clearly shocked. 'What? You have problems like this in Europe too?' I had their attention!

I began to tell them a bit of the history of Wales and how we Welsh had always felt like second-class citizens compared to the English. I spoke about injustices that we had experienced in our past, at which point I knew who the Hutu were by their knowing nods. We have a proverb in Welsh, which when translated means 'Strike the wall so that the partition can hear,' meaning that often people can hear things better if referred to indirectly, and I later discovered that this is also Rwandan cultural practice.

I had total freedom to speak about my own country and I saw that they were identifying with me. I could then describe injustices which had similarities in Rwandan history and this became a very useful tool. They could open their hearts to me, feeling that I understood what it was like to belong to an oppressed people group. This Welsh background turned out to be significant not only in Rwanda but also in many other countries where there was conflict.

Chapter Eleven

FINDING HEALING AT THE CROSS

During the next few days, I met with various church groups and listened to the most terrible stories imaginable. I wondered what I could possibly say that could begin to heal these enormous wounds. God gently prodded my heart: 'What healed you (and continues to heal you) of the wounds caused by life's hurts?'

'A revelation of Your heart,' I replied. 'The more I see Your character and the more I understand Your ways, the more I get healed.'

Although there was no comparison between my wounds and theirs, I felt that probably the principles would be the same, so hesitantly I began sharing some of the key principles that brought healing to me. And, to my amazement, the people responded with: 'These teachings can heal us! This is what the whole country needs!'

Something I learnt much more about in Rwanda is that the cross is the place of healing wounds as well as forgiving sin. I was sitting with a group of Pentecostal pastors in Nyamata towards the end of that first visit. I remembered the UNHCR workshop in Liberia (see chapter 8) and wondered if that could work in this horrendous situation, but this time from a Christian perspective. I decided to give it a try.

I encouraged them to write on a piece of paper what they had experienced and what they had seen done to someone else. Then I encouraged them to meet in small groups of two or three to share the horrors they had experienced and witnessed, and pray for one another. This was hard for them, but reluctantly they agreed. Later, when they returned to the big group, they began to feedback what they had written and my translator recorded the statements on a wall chart.

I was appalled by what I heard: the participants had seen their loved ones hacked to death by machete; pregnant women ripped open and the babies butchered; others buried alive or impaled on wooden spears. I could hear laughing as these terrible stories were shared and I could hardly bear it, even though I understood that culturally this was the only emotion they were free to exhibit.

I wondered what on earth I should do next and frantically asked God what they could possibly do with all this pain. Immediately the answer came: it must all go to the cross. There was nowhere else that it could go. Isaiah 53:4 came to my mind. *'Surely he bore our griefs and carried our sorrows.'* Not only our sin – our griefs and sorrows too.

When the writing was finished I asked them what they thought God felt about what was written. The laughing stopped instantly. 'Pain,' they said, 'terrible pain.' I asked them if they were going to carry these horrors in their hearts for the rest of their lives.

I told them that I knew of only one place where this could be taken. Seeing a red marker pen on the table I picked it up and silently walked to the wall chart, drawing a large red cross through the middle of the writing.

I could hear the room hush behind me and then those 'Tt' sounds again. I remembered my experience with the abused woman on the course we were running in North Wales. 'Everything written here has already been transferred to Jesus on the cross,' I said. 'He not only carried our sin – He carried all the consequences of sin. The whole tragic human condition was there. Only a crucified God is big enough to carry all this pain.'

I urged them to pour out their hearts to Jesus and by faith see all that pain being transferred to Him. If we hold onto our pains and don't give them to Him, Jesus will have died in vain where this is concerned. Some began to wail loudly, others silently wept. After some time, when the wailing was dying down, someone began singing in their own language,

> *What a Friend We Have in Jesus,*
> *All Our Sins and Griefs to Bear*

– the very same hymn they had sung at a similar point in Liberia. One pastor said, 'I've sung that hymn all my life. It's only today that I understand what it means.' It was clear they were experiencing some kind of relief. I was so grateful.

I then suggested we should also look at the good things. 'Are you crazy?' their faces asked, 'We've just survived a *genocide*!' I asked them if there was anything good that God was doing in the midst of the darkness.

One or two hands went up and I heard stories of incredible heroism and bravery and of people coming to faith in the midst of the suffering. 'There are many new believers in Rwanda today,' they said, 'because they saw how true believers die. People died with the Holy Spirit upon them!' I was intrigued and asked to know more. They told me that some people were singing, others were praying a blessing on their killers. This touched me deeply.

Once they got the idea, more and more moving stories were told, for example, of Hutu who risked their lives hiding their Tutsi friends, and sometimes died doing so. I heard of the militia arriving at a church meeting, telling all Hutu to leave as they were only interested in Tutsi. No one moved. They were given repeated warnings and opportunities to leave but refused. 'We are all children of God here,' they said. 'If anyone is to die, we'll die together.' And that's what happened. Over the next few years, I heard several similar stories.

Eventually there was a long list on another wall chart. In fact, this list was longer than the list of sufferings. 'Do you realise you have just proved John 1:5 to be true?' I asked. *'The light shines in the darkness and the darkness could not overpower it.'* Even the worst darkness that any country could experience had failed to extinguish the light of God's love. And if Satan had failed to extinguish the light in Rwanda, he would surely not succeed anywhere else.

At this, there was great rejoicing. The drums came out and people started worshipping. Later, the senior pastor told me that from now on whenever he remembered the horror, he would also remember the good things that God was doing. That would change everything.

THE CENTRALITY OF THE CROSS

Later, this exercise became the centre of a three-day healing workshop. In order to make it more realistic, a rough wooden cross was made, and the participants were invited to come and nail their stories to the cross. It was a bit of a struggle to persuade some denominations to use a wooden cross, as they thought we might be making an idol out of it. So I had to point to the use of symbolism in the Bible. The story of the blind man and the pool of Siloam in John 9 was useful. Jesus put clay on his eyes and told him to go to wash in the pool. There was nothing special about the clay or the pool, but Jesus evidently knew that helping this man to act something out would help his faith to grow to the point where he could receive his healing. This reassured them.

For other denominations, the use of the cross was particularly helpful. When we arrived at a Catholic centre to run our first workshop for Catholics, the nuns confessed afterwards that they had been very suspicious and uneasy about meeting with Protestants, but when they saw us carrying a cross, they were reassured. 'The cross will bring us together,' they said. Yes!

After nailing the papers to the cross, some were anxious about what would happen to them and who might read them. So I suggested we carry the cross outside and burn the papers. This became an important part of the whole workshop. 'This is like a burial,' they said. 'We are going to bury our pains.'

The burning of the papers was always a poignant time. People would look wistfully at the papers and several remarked, 'As surely as the smoke is rising, God is receiving my pain in heaven.' And I hardly remember a time when they didn't spontaneously burst into songs of praise once the papers were all burnt.

After the burning, all that remained was a pile of ashes. Once I had learnt about the fire lilies, I would describe them at this point, telling them how I had seen these beautiful flowers growing out of the ashes.

After one session at the cross, I saw the next morning that someone had put some red flowers into the ashes. I thought it was a great idea and from then on that also became an integral part of the whole ceremony.

Nailing their pain to the cross

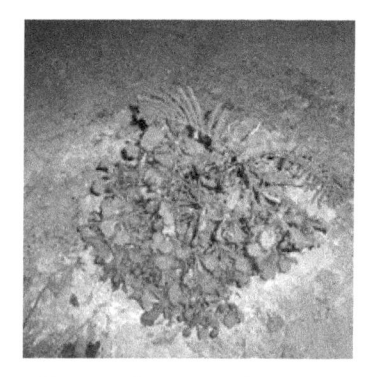

Putting flowers in the ashes

I would ask them if they believed that God could bring something beautiful out of these particular ashes. If so, and if there were plenty of wildflowers in the vicinity, they were to go and find a flower and put it into the ashes. (In later workshops, if there were no flowers nearby, the team would go to buy some; but if they were out of season, we would carry some artificial red flowers with us.)

For me this is one of the most touching parts of the whole workshop. I have seen hundreds of piles of ashes totally covered with flowers. This is such a sign of hope. Believing that God can bring some meaning out of our suffering and actually use it for good in some way, brings such healing.

After placing the flowers in the ashes, we would hold hands in a circle and would pray all together for the person on the right and on the left that God would bring something beautiful out of the suffering they had given Him that day. Sometimes singing and dancing would break out spontaneously at the end, often going on for quite a while, before we gave God's peace to one another. In some workshops, this time of rejoicing went on well into the night, with people complaining of being hoarse the next morning because they had sung so much.

Wherever the Cross Session was carried out, the next morning would be full of joy. To my amazement, people would be queuing up to tell of the change that had taken place in their hearts the previous afternoon. Many had slept peacefully for the first time since their terrible experiences. I heard things like, 'Until yesterday afternoon, not only did I hate those who killed my family, but I also hated the whole tribe. Today I feel very different. I'm now ready to forgive.'

I asked them what had made the difference. 'Well, you encouraged us to give our pain to Jesus,' they said, 'And we did! Now our hearts are free to forgive. It's very hard to forgive while your heart is still full of pain.'

Before wounded people can be healed, they must first face and express their *Pain*

Ability to forgive

Isaiah 53:4

Through this I learnt a very important lesson. True forgiveness requires the cross. It did for God and I believe it does for us too. It taught me that it is better not to teach on forgiveness until people have first been to the cross. The anger that prevents forgiveness can only be diffused by addressing the pain beneath the anger, and the cross is the place we find healing from that pain. By now, we have realised that the cross must be central to all we do and in fact, is the place of greatest healing for *all* of life's wounds.

A NEW SEASON BEGINS

At the end of that first visit to Rwanda, those who had attended our meetings said that every pastor in Rwanda needed to hear this kind of teaching. 'You must come back,' they said, 'and take this message of hope right round the country.'

Two significant events occurred before my next visit to Rwanda. The first happened when I helped to run a 'Face to Face' course for missionaries held in North Carolina, USA. While there, we drove through Cherokee country and stopped to look round the memorial to their tragic 'Trail of Tears'. As I read their story, my heart said strongly that the place I wanted to be was with wounded, hurting people groups. Was God leading me into a new ministry?

Chapter Twelve

THE *HEALING THE WOUNDS OF ETHNIC CONFLICT* WORKSHOP IS BORN

(The name has now changed to Healing Hearts, Transforming Nations *– see chapter 22. See Appendix Two for details on the workshop sessions.)*

'You have no permission to conduct workshops here! Only those specifically trained by the UN are allowed to speak to traumatised people.' But the whole country of Rwanda was traumatised. Even though I assured them I was a Christian, teaching the Bible to Christians, it was only when I showed them my psychiatric qualifications that they reluctantly allowed me to start conducting meetings there.

I remembered the strong impression that my pastor had received that I needed to qualify as a psychiatrist as it would someday open doors that would not otherwise open. It really had been God's guidance after all.

God's strategy was becoming clear in my mind. He would use the church as an agent of healing and reconciliation in the country. Those who loved Jesus, whatever their denominational background, would join together to be the agents of God's healing. My Rwandan friends got excited with this vision.

But how could a diseased church heal anyone? As the church had been part of the problem, the government was dubious that it could now be part of the solution. Returning to Rwanda in 1995, it was obvious that the church would first need to be healed. So how would we go about this? 'Let's run a workshop,' they said, 'and call together Christian leaders from all the denominations. Then we will ask God to heal us and change our thinking.' But then they thought it would be too difficult to bring different churches together. 'You'll have to go to each denomination separately,' they suggested. I was grieved in my spirit.

This was the legacy of missions. We had not only brought Jesus to people, but we also brought our structures and systems. We brought the same divisions that we were experiencing at home. Working with each denomination separately would take a hundred years, I thought. And anyway, it's the united Body of Christ that can heal this nation. I clearly needed to apologise on behalf of Western mission for bringing them a divided Gospel.

'Let's try,' I said. Being told that 'nothing can be done' reminded me that this is what my father used to say when we needed solutions to the family's problems. Years later I discovered that something could have been done and this led to a strong motivation not to accept negatives at face value. It means I can be very stubborn in the face of discouragement or being told something is impossible. I have a strong desire to prove them wrong. I can see now that my painful teenage years are being used for good.

'For how long can I bring people together?' I asked. 'Oh, no longer than three days,' they said. 'These church leaders are busy people. They would never agree to come for longer than that.' 'Okay,' I said, 'let's plan for three days.' But then I started to panic. Three days? Clearly it was impossible for any human being to do anything, especially in three days! I started to pray desperately. 'Lord, You have to come Yourself into our midst. This is going to take a miracle and only You can work miracles.' I also sent out prayer requests to many prayer partners in different parts of the world, asking them to pray for God's presence to be very real and for people to begin (at least) to experience significant healing and be able to leave the workshop looking at the other side through new eyes. Looking back, God must have given me a gift of faith for that.

So the invitations went out and, to everyone's surprise, each denomination in the locality was represented.

And from the beginning, we saw God at work so powerfully, in ways that far exceeded my expectations. This must have been made possible by the prayers of many unknown people all over the world praying for post-genocide Rwanda. I want to emphasise that from the start, it was local Christians at the grassroots who responded to the message. We were all who the world considers as 'nobodies' working together – a situation that appears to delight God (1 Corinthians 1:26-29).

At that first meeting with Christian leaders in Kigali, there was little interest in taking things further: in many ways this was understandable as Europe was certainly not viewed in a favourable light in those days. And, after all, who was I? Just an unknown Christian woman, who had flown in from a comfortable life in Europe. I hadn't gone through the horror they had just gone through. What credibility did I have to speak to anyone? The only person who showed an interest was Antoine Rutayisire, at that time the national leader of African Evangelistic Enterprise.

Maybe Antoine's previous connection with Wales helped as well as his high respect for several of my friends there. He was happy for our ministry to become part of that organisation. The need for reconciliation was in his heart as he had worked hard before the genocide to try to promote urgent prayer as he sensed that dark clouds were gathering.

Sadly, people were fatalistic and passive, believing that the known prophetic message about 'rivers of blood flowing' in Rwanda described something that could not be prevented. With hindsight, many now recognise that this had been a warning from God to get His church to rise up and take action. Tragically the genocide against the Tutsi overtook their attempt to bring the church to urgent prayer.

Nevertheless, I believe that Antoine's efforts were not wasted. Maybe it's only in eternity that we will know what his prayers accomplished. After the genocide, Antoine continued to have a prophetic voice in the nation, calling people to reconciliation. Antoine's full story can be read in his challenging book, *Reconciliation is My Lifestyle*.

I also believe that those who laid down their lives to try to bring peace and reconciliation there, gave us a head start. Their death was not wasted. Israel Havugimana, the first leader of African Evangelistic Enterprise, a Hutu, was one such person. He was one of the first people to be killed when the genocide broke out. We were starting this work 'standing on the shoulders' of men and women like Israel, and coming from that organisation, his testimony gave credibility to our work.

EARLY STRUGGLES

Nevertheless, starting these workshops was not without struggle and pain. By this time, Medair (see chapters 8 and 9) had left the country as the relief organisations were so numerous that they were almost falling over each other. So Medair decided to move their focus to Sudan. But before doing so, they had partnered with African Evangelistic Enterprise, who agreed that I should return and work under their auspices.

Life was extremely challenging for any local organisation seeking to work in post-genocide Rwanda. Everyone was traumatised and trying to survive in the face of enormous physical and emotional or mental needs.

It seemed there was a misunderstanding about what I would do there and when I returned in 1995, they had arranged for me to work with different orphanage staff and others seeking to work with traumatised children. I had not brought any materials with me for this purpose and it was a very difficult time for me.

In the meantime I also spoke in various meetings and churches. During that time, there were Scriptures that became very precious to me. Isaiah 25:6-9 speaks of a mountain where God will destroy the shroud – the sheet over a dead body – that covers all nations and He would swallow up death forever. I know of only one event where that took place – the death and resurrection of Jesus. It also speaks of a rich banquet being prepared for *all* nations, a wonderful promise foretelling the 'wedding feast of the Lamb' in the book of Revelation.

Isaiah 60:1-3 speaks of God's glory coming upon His people in the midst of thick darkness and eventually nations coming to the light of His people. There was very little light at that time but I felt God asking me to have faith to read these Scriptures prophetically over Rwanda wherever I spoke, believing that one day the nations would come to learn from Rwanda.

My heart was to work with the church, but the leaders of the organisation were so busy that it was hard for them to find time to discuss things with me. Only near the end of my visit did I eventually manage to share my vision with them. They then readily agreed and proceeded to arrange a workshop for Christian leaders.

But how should such a workshop be conducted? There were already many secular and Christian groups offering trauma healing. Would we simply be duplicating what others were doing? I knew some were experiencing difficulties. I heard that people were unresponsive, unwilling to talk and share their pain, as this was against their culture. When someone preached about forgiveness, people got angry.

'Don't you realise how much I've suffered? I've lost my whole family! And you're saying I should *forgive*?'

RUNNING THE *HEALING THE WOUNDS OF ETHNIC CONFLICT* (HWEC) WORKSHOP

Praying about this, I felt it was very important to hear from God what the content and sequence of the workshop should be. Not having come with any pre-arranged Western programme, I was thrown onto utter dependence on God, to show the way through the workshop. I wondered how I could address the terrible losses in Rwanda without being political and apportioning blame.

I decided that they needed to know the bigger picture, that as human beings we all have a common enemy who is seeking to destroy us. John 10:10 was a very useful scripture, telling us that the Thief (Satan) has come to kill, steal and destroy, but that Jesus has come to give us life, and life in all its fullness. They were very ready to make a list of the things that the Thief had stolen from Rwanda. We concluded that the most significant thing we have been robbed of is truth, especially truth about a loving, just God.

Unless we knew the real God, we had no hope of being healed. It was clear that a good foundation would have to be carefully laid before people could risk opening up their heart wounds. The only sure foundation is the love of God and we would have to start there and then go step by step as the Holy Spirit led.

I was shocked to hear people saying, 'God sent this genocide to punish us. We must be the most terrible people on earth!'

Clearly we would have to tackle this first. I don't believe that God sends any genocide, so understanding God's heart, His feelings and attitudes and how He felt about the genocide, became the foundation of the whole workshop.

FACING OUR DOUBTS

So, the rest of the first day was focussed on God's character, trying to see the interface between God's Sovereignty and man's free choice. I was learning even as I conducted the workshop. There was a debate about whether the genocide against the Tutsi had come from God or from Satan but it seemed that few were willing to say that it was our human responsibility.

I felt it was very important to focus on *our* part in humanity's sufferings and on a later visit I decided to take a string puppet with me. I pointed out how good this puppet was. It never disobeyed me, never did anything wrong. Is this how God had made us? If not, why not? If we never did anything wrong, there would be no genocide, no injustice, no one wounding anyone else. Some suggested that maybe God should have made us this way, but others disagreed, saying that they didn't want to be robots.

Next, it was important to discover why God chose not to make us robots. Eventually, after much interesting dialogue, we would arrive at the conclusion that God created us for a love relationship. Robots can't love, because love always has to be a choice. This was so important to God that He was willing to take the huge risk that we would all make the wrong choices. The tragedy is that this is exactly what we did.

I shared with them what God had shown me during my time with YWAM, regarding His pain expressed in Genesis 6:6, where God even regrets having created human beings with the freedom and dignity to make their own choices. Only His relationship with Noah convinced Him not to call it a day and bring all of creation to a premature end.

Understanding something of God's pain was significant for their healing. I found the Scriptures from Luke 13:34 and 19:41-44 very helpful for this. We could hear Jesus' pain that although His desire was lovingly to protect the people of Jerusalem as a mother hen does her chicks, they were not willing.

I substituted Rwanda for Jerusalem: 'Oh Rwanda, Rwanda…' (Since then many other countries have found their way into that verse.) Then we see Jesus weeping over the city, knowing what the consequences of their refusal to listen to Him would be and obviously heart-broken about it. I was careful not to suggest that people were responsible for their own suffering. In that verse, I believe Jesus is referring to the leadership. When unjust leaders in a nation refuse to listen to God, many innocent people suffer.

We sought to answer the very question the prostitute in Amsterdam had asked: 'If it wasn't God's will, why didn't He stop it?' I turned the Amsterdam experience into a short drama. Someone approached an innocent victim carrying a weapon. We asked what God should do if He loved this innocent person and they suggested the various things God could do.

In the end, they concluded that He couldn't have carried out any of their suggestions, or there wouldn't be anyone left alive, or we would all be paralysed and so on. When we enact this little drama now, we always hope that someone will say, 'He could have used someone else to rescue him.' 'Now we're talking,' we say. 'How does God usually like to work in the earth?' 'Through us,' they respond. We suggest that, when the people of the world are shaking their fists at God asking, 'Where were You?' if we listen carefully we may hear a voice from heaven cry, 'Where were *you*?' Many are regretting today that they didn't take an active role in protecting their neighbours from harm.

I will never forget running a modified workshop with a group of Tutsi children in an orphanage run by a lovely Charismatic Catholic lady. When discussing the question of what God should do when people do evil things, I asked them if they thought God should have killed the killers before they killed their parents. I expected them to say 'Yes!' They were thoughtful for a few minutes and then agreed that the answer was 'No.' 'Why not?' I asked. 'That would make God no different from the killers,' they explained, 'and anyway, those killers need the chance to repent.' I was amazed and deeply moved.

People often point out that there *were* some miracles when God intervened to rescue some people. But why so few? Some suggest it's because people didn't have enough faith. But Hebrews chapter 11 refutes that notion. After describing how by faith many experienced miraculous rescues, it goes on to describe many who didn't. Verse 39 doesn't say, 'Those who were not rescued lacked the faith for a miracle.' Rather it says, '*These were **all** commended for their faith*' (bold letters mine). I felt it was very important to stress that those who were not rescued did not have less faith and were not loved any less than those who were. *'Precious in the eyes of the Lord is the death of His saints'* (Psalm 116:15).

It was crucial to end in a place of hope and to remind ourselves that God is a redeeming God who can even turn our loss into gain. In the early days, I was afraid to suggest this, but tremblingly asked if God could redeem even the Rwandan genocide against the Tutsi? 'Yes, He can!' cried one lady. When I asked how, she replied, 'We could show the world how to forgive.' Amazingly, this is now happening. Believing in redemption has become a strong key in our workshops. If God can turn our loss into gain, this gives us incredible hope even in the midst of great suffering.

BUILDING A HOUSE

In 1996 when I began to train the first local teams, God led me to the symbol of building a house to describe the sequence of the workshop. One never starts with the ceiling or roof. The foundation was a revelation of the heart of God. I believe this is the only foundation for true and lasting healing. Once we have seen what God is really like, it's safe to start building the walls, which are the healing of our inner wounds. It's only when we are sure of God's heart towards us that we can risk opening our wounds to Him.

The central part of this house is the cross. This is where the greatest healing and transformation can take place. Having encountered God's healing compassion at the cross, we can move to add the ceiling, which is composed of forgiveness and repentance. It's only when both those elements are present that reconciliation, our roof, becomes possible. This symbolic picture has been surprisingly effective in leading people through a process of healing and transformation. Each session builds on the previous one to prepare the heart for the next one. For this reason we always encourage people to come for the whole workshop, not just a part of it.

```
            Reconciliation
          Repentance
          Forgiveness
    ┌─────────────────────────┐
    │ H              †      W │
    │ e                     o │
    │ a                     u │
    │ l                     n │
    │ i                     d │
    │ n                     s │
    │ g                       │
    │ Revelation of God's Heart│
    └─────────────────────────┘
```

STAYING IN A LOCAL HOME

On my second visit to Rwanda, I had been placed in a Guest House, but I longed to be able to stay with a local family. Towards the end of my time there, I was delighted to meet some Rwandans who worked with YWAM. Immediately I knew that this is where I wanted to stay next time, as I had experienced YWAM's values and vision. I asked them if that would be possible, but they were very hesitant, saying their house was no place for a European. They gave me various reasons why they didn't think it would be suitable: 'We have rats!' they said, 'and the only water in the house is what comes through the roof. And there are bullet holes in the doors and we have no bathroom. The toilet is outside and is a long-drop…' But I pleaded with them to let me try, so in the end they agreed that I could stay with them on my next visit.

I can't be grateful enough for that decision. They became like family to me and I loved being with them. They accompanied me to several workshops and helped me run them. But the best thing was that I got to understand nuances and cultural beliefs that many other foreigners had not picked up even though they had been living there for years. I was so blessed when their young daughter, on hearing me being called a *muzungu* (white foreigner) was aghast.

'Rhiannon is not a *muzungu*!' she remonstrated. 'She's *our* Rhiannon.'

A year later, Kristine Bresser, an American friend, joined me. She had volunteered in Rwanda with a division of Mission Aviation Fellowship UK and had hosted Methode and Mary Kamanzi, the YWAM leaders, in her home for a while. Although the situation in the country was still very sad with many wounded people around, we also had some real fun times staying with this family. The children were lovely and we often played board games with them, as well as with the extended family.

Rat catching was a favourite activity for them, when they all chased the rat with brooms and any available weapon. There were squeals of delight during the chase. I didn't share their joy! Kristine and I had twin beds in a very small bedroom. I remember Kristine waking me up with a cup of tea one morning, saying, 'Don't move too quickly. Do you see that bag at the bottom of your bed? There's a rat inside it.' She said afterwards that she had never seen me move so quickly.

One day Methode came home from a European trip with a gift for the family – a painting of Jesus. I was grieved to see a pale-skinned Jesus with blue eyes and blonde hair. Their son David was only around five years old at the time and I remember his look of horror. 'Is Jesus a *muzungu*?' I reassured him that Jesus was not white. He was brown, from the Middle East, and was in the middle between black and white, bringing us all together.

Chapter Thirteen

THE HWEC WORKSHOPS DEVELOPS

One of my main goals for conducting this workshop was that people would begin to have hope for the future. In spite of its failure, the church was still God's hope as an agent of transformation in the nation. That's true in every nation, even if the believers are in the minority. Jesus spoke of the Kingdom of God being like a mustard seed, the smallest of all seeds, yet it grows into a tree that can shelter the birds (Matthew 12:31).

He also compared His people to the light and salt of the earth (Matthew 5:13-16). Very little salt is needed to be effective in changing the taste of a large quantity of water. When I told them of God's hope in them, they shook their heads. 'No,' they said. 'We have lost our credibility. There's nothing we can say now. The government is saying that the church was part of the problem, so it can never be part of the answer.'

I felt a righteous anger stir within me, as I recognised what Satan's strategy had been against the church. By using the sin of some, he had sought to silence the whole. It seemed the whole church was now covered in a cloak of shame and this would have to be removed. They were the only ones with a message that could bring true and lasting healing and transformation. I prayed a very short prayer with which I am very familiar and strongly recommend: 'Lord, help!'

I remembered Jesus returning to His disciples after His resurrection (John 20:19-21). He did not come to a victorious group. They were heart-broken, defeated, having lost their Saviour and vision for the future; they were hiding behind closed doors and planning to return to their previous careers.

'How did He approach them?' I asked. Did He say: 'You failures – such a disappointment to Me! You had been my hope! I invested three years of My life in you and just look at how you behaved in a crisis! Clearly I'm going to have to work with angels, not humans, in future!' They began to smile and shake their heads. 'No,' they said. 'He started with *"Peace to you!"*' 'That's right,' I said, 'and He said it twice so they would really get the message! And this is also what He's saying to you.'

I went on to explain how He followed that greeting with something very remarkable. *'As the Father sent me, so I send you.'* That meant He hadn't changed His plan. He still believed in them. They were still to be the light and salt of the world. He was going to breathe His Spirit into them and that would change everything.

THE HWEC WORKSHOPS DEVELOPS

I then asked them to light a candle and pass it round the room as each said to the next person, 'You are the light of the world. You are the hope of this nation. God believes in you.' It was wonderful to see hope returning to their faces as they did this. All the darkness in the world cannot extinguish the light of even one small candle. It's the light that banishes the darkness.

LEARNING AS I WENT ALONG...

One of the ways to instil hope at the start of our workshops was through music and this is where my love of music and worship came in very useful. I also love learning the songs of another culture and singing in another language. We felt it important to begin each workshop with a significant time of worship and also to use it to make declarations of faith in what God was going to do in the nation. They have so many lovely worship choruses in Rwanda so our work was made easy. 'Urwera' is a beautiful song, which tells of God's glory being over the whole earth. We would sing this song over each town in Rwanda in turn, declaring that God's glory would be experienced there.

Another song which I grew to love was '*Kungoma*'. This declares that God is reigning on the Throne and has swallowed up death completely. Again, we sang this over each town in Rwanda. It was especially effective to repeat this song at the end of the Cross Session.

As always, I was learning as the workshop proceeded. I discovered it was important to teach the concept of 'woundedness' as some pastors were saying that being wounded was a sin.

I had to explain that being wounded was a valid Biblical concept for which God has great compassion. He takes our woundedness every bit as seriously as our sinfulness, and Jesus died to deal with both. In Jeremiah 30:12-13 we read that, humanly speaking, healing deeply wounded hearts is impossible, but we can rejoice that in verse 17, God says, *'But I will restore you to health and heal your wounds.'* In every country we have worked in, there is a history of unhealed wounds and unresolved conflict. Whole nations can have a wounded spirit. It was clear that the need for the healing of inner wounds would have to be a major emphasis in our workshops.

I now believe that unhealed wounds cause many, perhaps even the majority, of the problems we face in the world, both personally and at every level of society.

It is interesting that in Psalm 139:24, which asks God to search us to see if there is any wicked, or hurtful way in us, the literal Hebrew is 'see if there is any *painful* way in me.' Perhaps the greatest hindrance to our healing is our unwillingness to accept the pain within. We prefer to try to forget about it, thus suppressing it, which can cause all kinds of disease of spirit, mind and body. But God is longing and waiting to be gracious to us and to show us His compassion (Isaiah 30:18).

While I was sharing the need to have our inner wounds healed, and the resistance we often feel, one pastor said, 'Oh – it's like the story of Lazarus!' I was a bit puzzled and asked him to explain. 'Jesus came to heal Lazarus but when He got there, there was a big stone in front of his tomb. When Jesus told them to move the stone, Martha said, "Don't do that – there's a bad smell behind that!" We do that too when we have pain in our hearts. We put a big stone in front of it and don't want to move it because there's a bad smell behind it. But if we want Jesus to heal us we must be willing to move the stone away.' I was very impressed by his insight, and decided to use that example whenever I taught on woundedness.

I returned to Rwanda many times, staying a couple of months at a time, then going home for a break before starting again. My translator and I took the workshop to every town in Rwanda, returning in a few months to conduct a follow-up.

We wanted to know what the impact of the workshop had been – in their own lives, in their families, in their churches and in their communities. What we heard was so encouraging. God was evidently at work and miracles were taking place.

We heard stories of shocking forgiveness and reconciliation. I could write several books full of amazing testimonies. People had gone with supportive friends to visit the killers of their relatives in prison to convey their forgiveness, even inviting their families for a meal! Some asked if I could go to the camps in DR Congo where the Hutu (many of them guilty of taking part in the genocide) were sheltering in the surrounding countries, so that they could also be healed. As Tutsi, they used to hate them, but now they wanted to bless them.

PASTOR ANASTASE

By this time, I had a second translator, Pastor Anastase Sabamungu, a friend of the YWAM family with whom I lodged. He was a Tutsi who had grown up as a refugee in Uganda and had lost several relatives in Rwanda during the genocide. It became obvious very quickly that he was more than a translator and I began to encourage him to teach some sessions himself, which he did very competently. He was a great blessing to the workshop, having a compassionate, tender, pastoral heart. I was amazed that, with his history, he was still able to warmly embrace the Hutu in the workshop and to teach on forgiving. This was put to the test in one workshop.

We were in Bugesera where many Tutsi had been killed. In that workshop, a man stood up during the repentance time and said, in tears, 'I want to confess that my relatives took part in the killings and I didn't do anything to save lives. Please forgive us!' No one moved. He kept pleading to be forgiven and I wondered why Anastase was sitting with his head in his hands, seemingly frozen to the spot. Usually he was so ready to get up and minister forgiveness. Come on, Anastase, I thought. We can't let this poor man stand there pleading and no one responding. I can't do it, because I didn't lose anyone here. I prayed urgently for God to intervene in some way.

After a while Anastase got up and I saw he was weeping. He slowly walked to the man and embraced him. I was so relieved. It was only afterwards that Anastase told me that this was the place where many of his family had been killed by being thrown into the river. 'I hadn't realised until today just how costly it is to forgive,' he said. 'First, in forgiving I had to be willing to bear the pain myself, before giving it all to Jesus.'

This taught me a powerful lesson about forgiving. On the cross, Jesus took into Himself the horror and resulting pain of all the world's sins. He *became* sin (2 Corinthians 5:21). God was able to forgive because Jesus absorbed all the sin of humanity into Himself, and all the pain. We are asked to forgive as Christ forgave us (Colossians 3:13). So as we forgive, we become willing to bear the pain of that sin, but we can only do that in the knowledge that we can transfer it all into the heart of Jesus.

A GRAVE IN AN ORCHARD

Often, follow-up sessions became times of further healing. In one follow-up in Kibuye, a beautiful area in the west on the shores of Lake Kivu, we shared together suggestions of how to help some of our workshop participants who were struggling with particular needs. One was the inability to visit certain places because of painful memories associated with that place. One of the trainees, a Hutu who was well respected in the area, confessed that he was such a person.

His son had risked his life, ferrying many fleeing Tutsi across the Lake to safety in DR Congo. Eventually he was caught and killed and his distraught father buried him in his special orchard, a place he loved and proudly managed. Since then he had not been able to visit his orchard, which had become neglected and seriously overgrown.

On discovering the orchard was only a couple of kilometres away, someone suggested, 'Why don't we go there with him right now?' So we jumped into the back of a truck and went there, following our friend through the overgrown orchard till we reached the spot when his son was buried.

Immediately, several of the trainees started to clear away the thick undergrowth covering the grave. Once it was cleared, we stood round the grave in a circle holding hands and thanked God for the courageous, self-sacrificing life of his son. We prayed for healing for the wounded heart of his father. And right there at that spot we proclaimed the goodness and redeeming love of God, asking that His presence would fill that orchard. We then sang Francis Rowley's hymn together, *'I Will Sing the Wondrous Story of the Christ Who Died For Me'* in Kinyarwanda, the Rwandan language. Finally we all embraced our brother.

He then announced that he was going to come back to his orchard and tend it until it was beautiful once again and he made a commitment that every fruit that grew there would be given to widows and orphans. It was all so moving – beauty coming out of ashes once again.

CHANGING SCENES

When the genocide against the Tutsi was brought to an end, many Hutu fled to neighbouring countries fearing that there would be mass revenge against them. In the camps, guilty and innocent were mixed together. There they experienced the horror of cholera and so many died.

When the one million refugees began returning home from the camps in 1996, we knew we had to go round the country again. It's one thing to forgive your neighbour when he is dying of cholera in another country. *It's another thing altogether to forgive when he returns to live next door.* This time we would need to invite the survivors and the returnees to attend the workshop together – a very daunting task. But it had to be done.

THE HWEC WORKSHOPS DEVELOPS

The start of the next batch of workshops was very tense. Often it was the first time for those on 'both sides' to sit together in the same room and you could almost cut the atmosphere with a knife. But, in each one, the breakthrough came when they went to the cross together. There was only one cross for both sides and they listened to each other's stories before kneeling together, nailing their own issues to the cross.

The joy at the end of the session was unbelievable, the singing often continuing into the early hours. Again some were hoarse the next morning. I heard some very poignant responses.

'I thought my pain was the worst, until I heard my brother's.'

'I was amazed to see tears in the eyes of someone from the other side when I told my story! I never thought I would see this. But I was even more amazed to find that I had tears for him when I heard his story!'

My American friend, Kristine Bresser was a big help to me for the two years that she worked with me, especially on the administrative side.

Kristine and me

She made a particularly valuable contribution in transcribing the teaching as I spoke, putting this together as our first teaching book. Since then it has been revised numerous times and translated into many languages. Kristine has now specialised in debriefing training, working with Le Rucher Ministries.

DANGEROUS ROUTES

I will not forget many of our experiences during that time. We were invited to go to the north of Rwanda, where killings were still taking place. The British Embassy was advising against any travel outside of Kigali.

I met a Christian member of parliament in the Ministry of Justice and asked his advice. 'What can I say?' he responded. 'It's true there are very dangerous people up there. But this region needs your workshop more than anywhere. Let me make a suggestion. I can arrange an armed escort to accompany you.'

I took this suggestion back to the team. 'Are you joking?' they asked, 'How can we go to preach peace bearing guns! Anyway, the Lord of Hosts is with us. Why on earth would we need an armed escort!'

I told them I had not come to Rwanda to make widows of their wives and orphans of their children, so I sent them home to pray about it. I said that if anyone had any hesitation in their spirit, we would not go. To their great credit, they returned saying, 'We have to go. How else can this country be healed?'

THE HWEC WORKSHOPS DEVELOPS

So we went. We knew local people would be very suspicious of our visit and we always prayed during our journeys. I was so impressed with the team's prayers. I was expecting prayers like: 'Oh Lord, You know how dangerous this is! Please protect us! Please accompany us! Please help us!' Instead they prayed with great joy: 'Lord, we know You are with us! We praise you for your protection! We praise You for what you are going to accomplish!' We sang together most of the way.

When the local people saw us drive into the venue, they said, 'Everyone else is leaving but you're coming! Now we know that you're coming because you love us.' We discovered that where the danger was greatest, that's often where we saw the most fruit. When people are desperate, they take things more seriously. We witnessed amazing repentance, forgiveness and reconciliation taking place.

We returned there many times. Once there had been an ambush on the road there, with a minibus being burnt. Someone who had taken the initiative to promote reconciliation after attending a workshop had been on it. The atmosphere was poignant as we approached the spot where the minibus had been burnt.

I remember that the cassette tape in our vehicle was playing the sung version of St Francis of Assisi's prayer 'Make Me a Channel of Your Peace.' We could still see the ashes and we gave thanks for the life of our brother who had been martyred.

There was a song by Ron Kenoly that we frequently played on the vehicle cassette player, which gave us comfort, especially on dangerous roads.

> *Peace when trouble blows*
> *Jehovah sees, Jehovah knows*
> *He is my peace when sorrow nears*
> *Jehovah sees, Jehovah hears*

Once, we were staying down in the south of the country right at the border with DR Congo. While we were there, hostilities broke out between the two countries and we could hear guns and bombs going off in the distance. This was the first time I had ever been so close to active fighting. Amazingly I didn't feel afraid and suggested to the terrified workshop participants that we should have a time of praise. They looked a bit dubious but sang a song or two and then fled to their accommodation. The Rwandan army approached us and said, 'Tonight, there will be an exchange of fire and you are in a dangerous place. You must turn off all lights and sleep *under* your beds, not *on* them tonight.'

Later we could see tracer fire through the gap between the male and female sleeping quarters, but I was much more afraid of the creatures under the bed than of the bombs above it!

Kristine and I had a time of prayer and then read Psalm 91. *'No evil shall befall your tent.'* The mosquito nets above our beds looked just like tents, so we embraced that promise and went to bed.

Amazingly I slept well. We discovered the next morning that one missile had hit the cathedral behind us. After we got home to the UK, we learnt that a friend had been woken up that very night with an urgent burden to pray for our safety. I am convinced that the safest place to be is exactly where God wants us to be.

THE HWEC WORKSHOPS DEVELOPS

LE RUCHER MINISTRIES

Up to now, I had not belonged to any organisation, but had a small group of Christians in my home church advising me, to whom I was accountable. One day I received a letter from them saying, in effect, that my work was becoming a bit too hot to handle. I was going into dangerous places that they had no knowledge of and therefore could not give me sound advice. They urged me to find an experienced organisation which could better help me. I was devastated. I did not know of any other organisation doing the same kind of work.

Once again, God's timing was amazing. A few days later I was scheduled to visit my friends Erik and Jeltje Spruyt, who had been leaders in YWAM and had started a new ministry in Geneva called Le Rucher Ministries. This was a ministry mainly caring for the needs of missionaries, as well as enabling community development in various parts of the world.

When they realised my plight, they immediately invited me to join them and work under their auspices. This was such a God-given provision and blessing, as not only did they offer me accountability and considerable support in the work, but also debriefed me after I returned from challenging trips. I could never have continued working and seeing the ministry develop in many ways without their help over the 18 years that I worked with them. They also found a donor so that the work could continue under their oversight, after the funding dried up.

HOW WAS IT ALL FUNDED?

I have never fund-raised for my own personal finances or for the ministry. I always pay my own way. Friends and a few churches where I've been invited to speak, who believe in what I'm doing, have generously come behind me to support me and the ministry. But residential workshops are so much more effective than non-residential ones and that means expense. In post-genocide Rwanda, with all the breakdown in social structures, it was quite unrealistic to expect people to cover their own costs. Amazingly, usually in quite 'coincidental' ways that could only have been the hand of God, different large Christian charities have offered to support our work just when we needed it.

By now, we do ask participants to contribute what they can towards workshop expenses, as people will often take things more seriously if it has cost them something.

Chapter Fourteen

MULTIPLYING THE MINISTRY

The next priority was to hold training sessions so that others would be able to conduct this workshop themselves. Recognising that this ministry was the work of the Holy Spirit, we knew we could trust God to work through them as much as through us and maybe more. We were also aware that we needed a Hutu to complete the national team. Then we would be demonstrating what we were teaching.

In describing our ministry, I want to emphasise that we were by no means the only ones seeking to bring healing and reconciliation to Rwanda and we honour everyone else's contribution. For example, some helped Rwandans to overcome cultural resistance, enabling them to talk about their traumatic experiences; others trained counsellors; others brought communities together to engage in dialogue about their different perspectives.

When we met Joseph Nyamutera in a workshop in Gisenyi, Rwanda, on the northern border with DR Congo, we felt that he was the one to complete our team. Joseph, a Hutu, had been an English secondary school teacher there before the genocide against the Tutsi and was a committed member of the Pentecostal church. After the genocide was brought to an end, many Hutu feared indiscriminate reprisals and so fled the country to one of the surrounding countries.

Joseph (left) and Anastase at Le Rucher, 2006

Although Joseph had not participated in the genocide, he and his family fled to DR Congo with thousands of other Hutu. There they suffered greatly and he lost several members of his family to cholera, including his little boy. Conditions in the refugee camp were miserable, people sleeping on hard, craggy volcanic earth in makeshift tents.

A British relief worker in the camp arranged and paid for him and his family to fly to Kenya for him to enrol in a Bible College. Sharing out their shabby possessions, they left with great joy, but this dream ended abruptly when the Kenyan authorities in Nairobi refused them entry. In shame and disappointment they were flown back to the same camp.

Not long after this, the camps were dismantled and they made the journey on foot back to Rwanda, but his heart was full of pain and bitterness. This was still his condition when he attended a HWEC workshop, where he encountered God's love in a deep way, beginning a process of transformation. We recognised God's calling on his life and invited him to attend a training week in Kigali and afterwards to join the team.

After attending the mandatory rehabilitation camp, Joseph joined the team as a translator, but it became clear to me that both he and Anastase (Tutsi) were very capable teachers, so I transferred the workshop into their hands. God started to use them powerfully. Many would say that simply seeing them working together, was the start of their healing.

Having a Hutu and Tutsi teaching side by side also enriched our understanding of the history of Rwanda. I think it was Joseph who highlighted for us the significant and destructive role of prejudice. He says that when people seek to analyse the causes of the Rwandan genocide against the Tutsi, they come up with many suggestions, but hardly ever speak of prejudice. Yet he believes that the pre-existing prejudices were like land mines, waiting to be trodden on and exploded.

I remembered the power that prejudice had played in my own life. I grew up believing the English were all colonial Empire builders, who didn't care about anyone else's language or culture. They were all the same – they were arrogant and believed that they were superior. Whilst I had experienced negative attitudes from some English people, the mistake was in believing that *'they are all the same.'* That's the power of prejudice – through generalisation, it judges and condemns a whole people group.

We realised that identifying the prejudices and renouncing them was going to be an important part of our work in seeking to heal this land. All behaviour begins in the mind. What we think and believe determines the way we live. But how were we to address them when things were so sensitive? Again, my personal story came in useful in the workshop. It was no problem for me to explain my own prejudices against the English and our woundedness when it seemed to us that everyone else felt we were inferior to them.

Joseph confessed that many Hutu had believed the Tutsi were devious, not to be trusted. They were cockroaches and snakes. Years later whilst working in prisons with those convicted of genocide, he asked them how they had been able to even kill babies. Their response was shocking: 'Baby snakes are just as dangerous. They grow up to be adult snakes and so should also be killed.' Once we dehumanise our enemies, it's much easier to try to eliminate them.

Although his own parents did not teach him to have prejudice, later Joseph also came to believe these prejudices. He confessed, using humour to lighten the tension, his great fear that God would give him a Tutsi wife. Anastase also confessed that many Tutsi had grown up believing the Hutu were ugly gluttons, only fit for tilling the land; they were natural killers, definitely not to be trusted. It was clear that the divisions in the country had been very deep, so dealing with the prejudice was crucially important. It was so gratifying when participants began to thank them for saying the things that no one else dared to say.

At the end of training times, many were encouraged to form local teams to begin running the workshops themselves and Anastase and Joseph mentored them to help them do so. I thank God (and so does Joseph by now) that Joseph wasn't accepted into Kenya. God had a much better plan. Through this ministry, God is giving him a worldwide influence beyond anything he could have imagined. Another example of God's amazing redemption – gain coming out of loss, beauty coming from the ashes.

The teams now believe it's very important to work with children, youth and university students, so that they don't grow up with the same destructive prejudices.

ENCOURAGING THE TEAMS

I would return periodically to help them run forums where local teams came together for mutual encouragement. These were great times. The teams would greet each other like long lost families! The level of honest sharing of both struggles and successes was heart-warming. As well as seeking to give them uplifting Bible teaching, we always conducted another Cross Session for them. In this session they dealt with the pain they had heard and experienced while facilitating this workshop. It was essential for them to deal with anything that would reduce their effectiveness.

After some years, Anastase retired in order to focus on pastoring his growing church and Joseph took over the leadership of the ministry in Rwanda. These days he is part of the international team and is also invited in his own right to many parts of the world to teach and share his experiences. He also acts as consultant, helping struggling new teams.

FEEDBACK FROM THE TEAMS WE HAD TRAINED

I heard that the trained teams were surprised and thrilled by the way God was using them. They asked Joseph and Anastase to tell me that the Holy Spirit was with them just like He was with us. They were eager for me to meet some of the people who were being transformed through their workshops. So, I arranged to have two free days in Kigali during my next visit to Rwanda in 2006 when I could interview some of their workshop participants, and asked if they could arrange for the ones they chose to come to Kigali to meet me.

I will never forget those two amazing days. I listened to one 'walking miracle' after the other. I'll share with you about four people that made a deep impression on me.

FRANCOIS AND RENATA

As a Tutsi, Renata lost all but three of her entire extended family in the genocide. On top of that, she was raped several times and ended up suffering from AIDS. For ten years she was unable to leave her house, not trusting anyone, even her own group. Then someone from the local team that had been trained in her area (Gitarama) knocked on her door and invited her to a workshop that they believed could help her.

Renata was persuaded to attend and was struck by the message of Jesus being her pain-bearer. She was a believer and knew Him as her sin-bearer, but this was totally new to her.

She wrote out the outline of her story, but it took her a long time kneeling at the cross to be able to release her pain and nail her paper. She wept bitterly, but having nailed her paper she felt a lightness come into her spirit.

The next morning, during a time of repentance, someone stood up and confessed that he was the one who had killed her immediate family. She let out a cry of pain, but then remembered that she had put that on the cross the previous evening. 'God's mercy suddenly filled my heart,' she said. She got up, walked over to the man, embraced him and said to him, 'You are very courageous to confess this and I want you to know you are forgiven.'

She immediately felt a great joy filling her heart. 'This forgiving is wonderful!' she thought, 'I now want to forgive everyone!' One of the ones who had raped her had been repeatedly writing to her from prison, asking her forgiveness, but in anger she had ripped up every letter. After going home, she wrote to him to say she had at last been able to forgive him. 'I am now leading a new and happier life,' she said, 'and I have learnt to forgive whoever wrongs me. I am also seeking to help my fellow survivors to forgive. My physical health has also improved greatly since I forgave.' I was fighting tears as I prayed for her at the end of the interview, knowing I had witnessed a miracle.

The next person to come in seemed very subdued. He looked down at the floor, telling me his name was Francois. 'I killed many people,' he said. Slowly he began to tell me his story. He had grown up hearing much prejudice against the Tutsi, believing they were really bad people, so when the genocide began he joined the mob in a killing spree. However, after it was all over, he felt very guilty and handed himself in to the authorities and was put in prison. His guilt weighed heavily on him and he could find no relief.

Soon, the prisons were filled to overflowing and the government decided that anyone who confessed his wrongdoing could complete his sentence in community service. He readily confessed and was released, but could still find no relief from his guilt. Then someone knocked at his door and invited him to attend a HWEC workshop. Here he heard what he described as wonderful teachings, especially about the cross. This was new to him and during the Cross Session he took everything to the cross. He hammered very hard as he nailed his paper and told me he felt as if a hand came down from heaven and cleaned up his heart. 'It was amazing,' he said.

But he said what amazed him the most happened the next day. During the time of repentance, he had been able to publicly confess his sin and the lady whose family he had killed was actually present in the same workshop. He could hardly believe it when she walked up to him and forgave him. I suddenly remembered Renata's story – could this be the man who killed her family? I looked at his address and saw he was also from Gitarama. 'Was her name Renata?' I asked. 'Yes, that's the one,' he said. 'We came here together. We have a good relationship now. We are working together in the community, seeking to help both victims and perpetrators.'

All this time, he gave me no eye contact and kept his head bowed and I began to feel compassion toward him. I assured him that I had needed forgiveness too. I had not killed but I had hated. Without God's forgiveness in Jesus there was no hope for me either. *'Eh, murakose!'* (Thank you), he said. His head was still bowed. I assured him that we were now equal before God and he was my brother. *'Eh, murakose!'* but there was still no eye contact. I then asked him to look me in the eye, telling him that God's plans towards him were for good and not for evil, to give him a future and a hope (Jeremiah 29:11). *'Eh, murakose!'* but this time he grasped my hands and looked me in the eye.

How amazing God is. Unbeknown to them, the local team had invited both of them to the same workshop and the cross had healed and transformed them both. They readily agreed that I could print their story and also agreed to have a photograph taken together. But Francois still looked very sad. 'Come on, Francois,' I said, 'God has forgiven you and so has Renata. I think that merits a smile!' So he smiled and they both held hands, a simple sign of friendship in Rwandan culture.

A RIVER OF LIFE FOR RWANDA

Two men came in together to be interviewed and told me their story. Daniel was the leader of a local branch of a national Tutsi genocide survivors group. He lived in Ruhengeri in the north and he had attended a HWEC workshop, but was determined that nothing would touch him. But for some reason, he kept attending one.

It was in his fifth(!) workshop that he realised that his bitterness was keeping him in bondage and that he needed to be set free. He put all his anger and bitterness on the cross. On returning home, he arranged for the local team (which included Hutu) to conduct the HWEC workshop for his survivors group. It was a tough workshop with a lot of anger expressed, but at the end, they agreed to attend another workshop, this time with released perpetrators present.

The other brother in the interview (whose name I have forgotten) was leading a perpetrators group. He had killed and had served his sentence in prison, where he found a personal faith in God. He attended the workshop that Daniel organised.

At the beginning, the survivors were quite bitter and resisted mixing with those from the prison. One of the survivors said that though he wouldn't harm anyone from prison, in his heart he wished them dead. After the Cross Session, Daniel said he forgave them and started to be friendly toward the prisoners, but they feared and avoided him.

Eventually, however, Daniel was able to bring both groups together and they formed what they called a 'Unique Association' to start helping each other. They came together to cultivate a field for either a survivor or a released prisoner. They started contributing money so they could help any of them with a need. This Association grew to the point where they were putting their money together to buy livestock for their members. They were now living in peace with one another.

Both of them had beaming faces and it was a great joy to meet them. It was very obvious that they were the greatest of friends.

'We are alive now,' they said. 'We want to be a river of life flowing out to bless Rwanda.'

TRANSFORMING A WHOLE COMMUNITY

Following their training, some pastors from Gisenyi (now renamed Rubavu) began to conduct HWEC workshops and a significant work of healing began to take place. They also formed the first interdenominational pastors' forum in the town. In 2010, Joseph's brother, Jean Paul Mukunzi, having had further training in community development, began to call together those with healed hearts to seek to improve life in their community.

He says, 'I have tried to create transformed communities by forming reconciled groups that work together to creatively design and implement initiatives, to meet their basic needs related to poverty, health, education, relationship and the environment. After HWEC workshops, people have hope to work for a bright future for themselves, their families, and communities. God's accomplishments in the community are amazing, we are seeing what is written in Isaiah 61:1-4 happening in very wounded and vulnerable people's lives.'

The projects include helping people grow nutritious mushrooms to sell to support the poor; making clay ovens which require far less charcoal and keep warm the whole day for cooking meals; contributing money to give gifts of sheep and goats to the poor; forming a reconciliation drama group, reconciliation sports events and reconciliation clubs in the local schools; planting trees on barren hillsides and many other initiatives.

A few years later, some friends and I had the joy of visiting the region and witnessing these projects. When we arrived with the Kigali team, the Executive Secretary of Rubavu Sector came to greet us. She wanted to personally thank us for the message, which had changed hearts and had ended up transforming the whole community. I still get news from Jean Paul from time to time and it seems they are still going from strength to strength.

Chapter Fifteen

FINDING GOD AS A LOVING FATHER

On one of my early trips, I learnt that fathering in Rwanda was usually distant and could be rather harsh. Culturally they were expected to approach the father through the mother, not directly.

This is going to be a hindrance to their coming to God for healing, I thought. Remembering my experience with the teenage boy soldiers in Liberia, I introduced a session on knowing God as a loving father. It had not been part of the original workshop. I didn't realise at the time how foundational it would be.

As we explored God's original plan for family, we saw His desire for us to experience His loving father and mother heart through our earthly parents. When it was time for us to learn to put our trust in an unseen God, it would come naturally as we had already experienced His heart. When asked to reflect on their childhood, it was clear from most of their responses that this had not been the case.

MY OWN EXPERIENCE

Once again I found that sharing my own personal story gave them permission to own their pain. I shared that I had not found the relationship with my father easy. He struggled to show affection and never said 'I love you.' Our culture in Wales also made that difficult. We were afraid it would make the children proud. It was very important to my father that I was successful and he wanted me to be the best at everything.

I so much wanted his approval and tried hard to please him. One day, aged about 12, I came home from school, so proud that I was top of the class in mathematics, with 97%. His response was, 'So what did you do wrong? If you had done everything right, you would have had 100%.' I realise now that this left a message in my heart. 'You are only acceptable when you are perfect.'

At the age of 16, I found a personal faith in Jesus, but always felt that God was dissatisfied with me. I wasn't reading the Bible enough, praying enough, witnessing to others enough... Many years later, when I was in my forties, I attended a workshop where I was asked to write down what I thought God felt about me. I wrote, 'Disappointed.' Of course He is, I thought, because I'm not perfect.

I didn't realise that my experience with my earthly father had distorted my view of God until some years later when I attended another workshop. Here I was asked to make a drawing of how I saw myself. I drew – of all things – a generator! The workshop leader was surprised. 'Why did you draw that?'

'Because everything depends on me. I have to be there for everybody else but there's no one there for me.'

'Oh, but your Heavenly Father is there for you!' she exclaimed. She then called out one of the group to represent Father God. He stood at the other end of the room, smiling and stretching out his arms towards me. 'Come to me, Rhiannon. I love you!' But I found I was rooted to my chair, unable to move. I hid my head in my hands, feeling so unlovable. He kept calling to me, but I couldn't respond. Anxiously, he began to move towards me, but the leader wisely told him to stay back. 'We need to find out the cause of her difficulty,' she said, 'God does not force Himself on anyone.' She asked me to describe my earthly father. I described someone who couldn't show affection, was often angry, had unrealistic expectations of me, who couldn't handle the family crises we experienced...

'Now this is beginning to make sense,' she said. She then asked another man to come and stand directly in front of 'Father God.' 'Now tell him what you would have liked to have received from your father,' she suggested. It was hard to express it, but then the words started to tearfully pour out. 'I felt we never really got to know each other. You never once asked me how I was feeling about anything and especially how I was coping with the family's big needs. You never comforted any of us. When there was a crisis, instead of my being able to lean on you, you needed to lean on *me*. I needed a real father!' And so on...

'Do you now understand what's happening?' she asked. 'Every time you approach your Heavenly Father, your earthly father is blocking Him from view. It seems to me that your earthly father was unable to meet the deep needs of your heart. Do you think you could release him from the demands of your heart and forgive him?'

(The word 'unable' was really helpful. He did try his best, but it seems his own 'jug of love' was empty, so he had nothing to pour into us. Looking back now, I believe he did love us all very much, but was unable to show it.)

'Yes, I can.' I said, and the man representing my father sat down. 'Now why don't you come to the only One who can meet all those needs of the heart? To everything you longed for, He says, 'I AM.' He can make up for all the lacks you experienced. He's the perfect Father who loves you unconditionally and always has done.'

Very slowly I struggled out of the chair and began to walk towards him, but seeing his compassionate face, I ran into his embrace.

For a long time he held me, as the group prayed. I let go, thinking, 'At last, there's Somebody there for me!' Then I thought, why did I let go? And went into his embrace again. The wonderful truth is that with our loving Heavenly Father, we never need to let go. We can live our whole lives in His embrace. John 1:18 tells us that Jesus dwelt in the bosom of the Father, and in John 17:24 on His way to the cross He prayed that we would be with Him where He is. That's why He went to the cross – so that we could live in the Father's embrace. And that's the place where all our service to God should begin – serving Him joyfully because we *are* loved, not in order *to be* loved.

Sometimes we hesitate to acknowledge any lacks in our parents, fearing that we are dishonouring them, but our healing begins with owning the pain. I discovered that, after dealing with the pain, I was freed to remember the good aspects of my father. Many happy memories came to mind, and that's when I was able to truly honour him as God desires. But even if our childhood has been very painful, there is always something we can honour them for, if it's only because they gave us the gift of life.

TURNING MY STORY INTO A DRAMA

In the workshops, I don't just tell this story, but rather act it as a drama, and I'm amazed at how effective it is. Often people are deeply moved as they watch. It has now been modified so that all the teams can use this little drama. After the teaching session, we offer a practical time for people to process their wounds and lacks. A big red heart is drawn on a flip chart and people can come and write in the heart what they would have liked to have received from a parent. Men and women from the team stand to represent the Father and Mother heart of God. Anyone who would like a hug can come forward and receive one, as well as words of affirmation that the team believe God is giving them for that person.

This is a most healing time. There are more tears shed in this session than in the one dealing with the wounds of genocide. Even in Rwanda's no-emotion culture, pastors would often wail as they received a loving hug.

I remember a time we ran the workshop for a group of Catholic nuns. When we got to this point, Joseph was aghast. 'We can't hug nuns!' he said. 'Of course we can,' responded Anastase. 'They're just wounded little girls.' And again there were many tears as they received the Father's love. There's nowhere like the Father's embrace to find healing for wounded hearts. We discovered that this session was essential to prepare people's hearts for dealing with the wounds of their nation.

When Joseph started teaching this session, he very effectively adapted it to be relevant to the African situation. He usually begins with his own story. Having not received love from his own father, who didn't even remember his name among the many children, he didn't know how to be a loving father himself. Joseph admits that he was very harsh, often unkind to his wife, and that his children were afraid of him.

After receiving the Heavenly Father's love for himself during a HWEC workshop, he returned home to love his family. When he arrived home with his first ever gift for his wife, telling her he loved her, she was shocked. Later, she confessed she thought he was going to die! I have stayed in Joseph's home many times and I can testify that he is a changed husband and father. His wife and children have no doubt now that they are greatly loved.

RECONCILIATION BEGINS AT HOME

Many years later, I met with a militia group from DR Congo. These were all people who had killed and had even committed cannibalism. By the time I met them they had become believers and keen intercessors through the work of the local

Congolese team that we had trained. I asked how many had grown up feeling loved in their families. Not one hand was raised. I asked them what difference it would have made to Congo if they had grown up feeling loved. They cried out, 'No war!'

Another time in DR Congo, pastors came forward wailing loudly to receive the Father's love. 'Now we understand why our sons joined the militia,' they wept. 'We were unable to give them the love they needed.'

It's easier for someone growing up feeling unloved to pick up a weapon. The leaders concluded that healing a nation had to start with healing families and that their family life was generally so dysfunctional that they would have to run additional workshops focusing only on this topic.

The workshop was obviously leading to reconciliation between families, not just between conflicting groups. We heard many stories like Joseph's of people returning home to ask forgiveness of their partners, children, parents, and of transformed family life as a result. This has happened in every country where we have now worked. That gives me great joy.

Thomas Green from India, who attended the workshop in Rwanda, returned home to be reconciled with his father whom he had resented for many years. After that he began running workshops by himself between ethnic groups in India who are hostile to one another, especially in Manipur, and God is using him powerfully. He admits he could not do that had he not first been reconciled to his own father. Reconciliation begins at home.

Chapter Sixteen

SHOCKING FORGIVENESS

'If you don't forgive, you will go to hell!' I heard that this is what some Rwandan pastors were teaching people who had lost almost their entire extended family in the genocide. Deeply traumatised people were being further traumatised by this. Either they were angry: 'Don't you know how much we've suffered? How dare you tell us to forgive!' Or they felt very condemned. They were trying hard to forgive as Christians, but it just felt impossible. Clearly, teaching on forgiving the offender was going to be quite a challenge.

So I did not mention forgiving until the third day of the workshop, after they had put their pain on the cross. To my amazement, I discovered that they were often ready to forgive by that time, but we still needed to understand what true Biblical forgiveness is and what it is not. Isaiah 57:14 says, *'Build up, build up, prepare the road! Remove the obstacles out of the way of my people.*' This showed me that we had to start by acknowledging the resistance in our hearts and seek to deal with it. Having to forgive the offender feels so unfair. Isn't it cruel of God to ask us to forgive when we've been so wounded?

I believe that Biblical forgiving is one of the most misunderstood truths, both in the church and in the community. Some charities seeking to help abused people and children, stress that the one thing they must never do is forgive, as this devalues them and somehow makes the wrong right. But this is because they don't understand what Biblical forgiveness really means.

So we started by exposing all the misunderstandings about forgiving, especially stressing that forgiving does not condone the wrong, making it right. When God forgave us through Jesus on the cross that was not condoning our sinfulness.

Forgiving never makes wrong right. Wrong will always be wrong, and God takes it all very seriously. The cross shows us that forgiving is the most costly thing in the universe. There is nothing easy about forgiving. And it certainly is not forgetting. How could anyone possibly forget that they lost most of their family in a genocide?

THE USEFULNESS OF DRAMAS

We used several dramas in this teaching. People often respond more to a drama than to mere words and remember it for far longer. This is where my love of drama came in very useful and my love of spontaneity. Initially these dramas were put together on the spur of the moment in the middle of the workshop.

After seeing their effectiveness, they then became part of the workshop.

To emphasise that forgiving is not forgetting, I place a large black cloth over someone, covering their head completely. The cloth represents their wrongdoing, which can never be forgotten. That cloth is always there in my mind whenever I meet, or even think about them. People say, 'Forgive and forget,' but I could never forget it. Does that mean I would never be able to forgive?

Then God speaks to my heart. 'Where do I see your sin now? Do I still see you covered in your sin?' I realise that as a believer, God looks at me very differently, because He knows that I have put all my sin on the cross. Can I not do the same with this person's sin? So I remove the cloth and place it on a cross. Now that person becomes a human being again, with the possibility of changing. I have not forgotten what they did, but I'm remembering it in a different way. Many have found this simple drama very helpful.

Giving Jesus the responsibility for the offender and their wrongdoing is a significant key. As Christians we are hopefully very familiar with giving our sin to Jesus, trusting He has already dealt with it on the cross. The challenge which we often overlook is to also hand over to Him the sin of those who have wronged us. Of course that does not take away their own responsibility to repent of their wrongdoing, but it does free us to be able to release that person from our own judgment.

Having dealt with various obstacles and misunderstandings, we then focus on the fact that true Biblical forgiveness is always giving an undeserved gift to the offender. Can any of us say that we deserve God's forgiveness? We explore in more detail why it is that God asks us to forgive. Far from working against us, as we suppose, forgiving actually works for us. It's because God values us so much that He asks us to forgive. This sets our hearts free from bondage.

There is a drama that God seems to use the most to demonstrate this. In the drama a team member has a rope with which he/she pulls behind them someone who represents the memory of a person who has wronged them, whom they have no intention of forgiving. This affects every aspect of their life, preventing them from enjoying their food, having a good night's sleep and making any progress in life. Every step is exhausting.

Our workshops are very interactive and the participants are asked to help them get free. If someone says to simply let go of the rope, the team member would respond with, 'Just let go? Never! Don't you realise how bad this was? It ruined my life! Doesn't anyone have a better solution?' Eventually we discover that the only way to get free is by taking that memory to the cross and tying it there. If we don't do that, we will be forever bound to the one who has wronged us, giving them the power to continue destroying our lives.

This is the drama that convicted Daniel, the leader of the group of genocide survivors, mentioned in chapter 14. Usually the dramas are presented by the facilitating team, but when Daniel attended his fifth workshop, the team apparently decided to call some of the participants to play the parts. Daniel ended up being the one pulling the rope behind him. Through this, God spoke to him, saying this was exactly what he was doing to himself and this also applied to his group. Unless they forgave they would always suffer in this way. 'By the time I got to the cross, I was not acting,' he told me. 'I really put everything on the cross during this drama and by the time I got back to my seat, I was free.'

Some people (maybe all of us?) struggle with Jesus' teaching in Matthew 6:14-15, which tells us that if we do not forgive others their sins, our Father will not forgive us either. There have been times when I would like to have erased that verse! But it's important to understand what it means. Our heavenly Father is not a revenging God, saying, 'Rhiannon, if you don't forgive, I'm not going to forgive you either.'

Revelation 13:8 speaks of *'the Lamb that was slain from the creation of the world.'* The cross was already planned, God having already decided to forgive humanity before we were created. This forgiveness was made possible when Jesus died on the cross and, ever since then, the free gift of forgiveness has been offered to anyone who is ready to receive it.

So what does Matthew 6:14-15 mean? Another impromptu drama helps us understand this…

One of the facilitating team plays the role of someone who has been severely sinned against and has no intention of ever forgiving. A rope is tied around his/her arms indicating how bitterness of spirit keeps them in bondage. But this person is religious and goes to church every Sunday, praying the line from the prayer that Jesus taught us in Matthew 6:9-13: *'Forgive us our sins as we forgive those who sin against us'*. Another team member represents Jesus, standing at the cross, holding out a card with the word 'Forgiveness' written on it. But the offended one cannot receive it.

Jesus speaks to the victim asking him/her about the offender. He/she responds with feeling, 'I hate him! Let him rot in hell!' then immediately prays again, *'Forgive us our sins as we forgive those who sin against us.'* This is humorous, but the point is made. The problem is clearly not on God's side. Eventually, the victim agrees to accept the Holy Spirit's help to remove the rope and place it on the cross, which frees him/her to receive God's needed gift of forgiveness.

Our prayer is that at the end of this session on forgiving, people will be able to see that the command to forgive is God's loving gift to us. We damage *ourselves* if we don't forgive.

STORIES OF SHOCKING FORGIVENESS

After the workshops, people are often able to forgive in the most shocking ways.

I met Odette in Nyamata, on my first visit to Rwanda. This was only twelve weeks post-genocide and I remember this beautiful lady approaching me saying she wanted to be an ambassador of peace in Rwanda. I didn't know her story then.

I later discovered that as a Tutsi she had lost her parents, her husband and all but one of her children in the genocide, some in the most brutal ways. It took participating in several subsequent HWEC workshops before Odette was healed of her great pain, but she became a faithful workshop facilitator and has lived her forgiveness by adopting orphans so that she could care for them instead of her murdered children. But the adopted children were not from her own Tutsi group. They were Hutu orphans, from the very group that had killed her children.

She has also worked unstintingly to minister hope to widows, many of whom were severely traumatised vand suffering from HIV as a result of gang rape. Odette has the most radiant face, always with a beautiful smile. She could have been so different – she had every reason to become a bitter woman. I count her as one of my most precious friends.

Odette and me

During the genocide, Eliane, a Tutsi in the northern province of Gisenyi in Rwanda, was separated from her family while fleeing for her life and was offered a safe refuge by a Hutu neighbour. There was, however, a price to pay – she became his sex slave. She bore him children and was obliged to marry him, but confessed that she hated them all.

Many years later, when the justice system had recovered and was beginning to bring genocide criminals to trial, her husband could have received a heavy penalty. This was when Eliane attended the HWEC workshop. At the end, she announced that she was going home to forgive and love her husband. Eighteen months later, her husband attended a HWEC workshop and went home to ask her forgiveness.

It would be hard to meet someone more loving than Eliane now. She had so much love and wondered how she could express it as she was not gifted as a speaker, so felt ill-equipped to conduct workshops. She decided to go to the marginalised, despised Batwa pygmy group to remove their jiggers (small worms in mud floors that burrow into the soles of feet).

Eliane removing jiggers from a Batwa lady's feet

(The Batwa are the third people group in Rwanda, making up around 1% of the population.)

There is a team of them doing this now and her husband works with her. This humble act has led to so much reconciliation among the groupings in that town. This simple woman is now being approached to help resolve domestic conflicts and to help disabled people all over the country.

Pascal was a Tutsi who lost several relatives in the genocide. He joined the army so that he could kill as many Hutu as possible, but soon realised that those who acted this way were being court-martialled. He was frustrated and bitter when he attended a HWEC workshop, but amazingly met with God and was able to forgive.

When he went home, he saw someone who had killed his family, working in the fields doing community service and walked towards him. The offender saw him, was very frightened and started running away. Pascal ran after him shouting, 'Don't be afraid! I've forgiven you! I love you!', much to the amazement of those standing by. Now they are good friends.

Without our knowledge, Pascal decided to reach out to both victims and perpetrators, running the workshop for them. He had not been through a training session and had no money, but asked people to bring a handful of cassava, rice, or beans so that they could eat. He became a very effective mediator, also working between individuals in the community. He discovered that they also needed to come to the cross to be able to receive healing and heart change before they could reconcile. When we met him several years later, we were astounded at what he had achieved by God's grace. His story has now been made into a video called 'As we forgive' (www.asweforgivemovie.com).

How I thank God for the beautiful fire lilies growing out of the ashes of devastation as people find the ability to forgive and become agents of reconciliation in their communities. By now I could tell you of so many more such testimonies in Rwanda and in different parts of the world.

Of course, forgiving is not a once for all experience, especially if the wrongdoing still continues and there has been no justice. In asking Peter to forgive seventy times seven, Jesus was teaching that forgiving must become a lifestyle. And it is an act of the will, not a feeling.

I personally find the statement that 'forgiving is a process' unhelpful. Too often, we can use that as an excuse to hold onto our anger. Getting to the point where we are able to forgive may be a process and living out our forgiveness will definitely be a process, but forgiving itself is clear-cut. We have either forgiven or we haven't. I have seen people forgive the most heinous of crimes in a moment, then proceeding to live their forgiveness. Sometimes that is very costly, especially if their family or people reject them, perceiving their forgiveness to be an act of betrayal.

Jesus' teaching to Peter suggests not a process but making repeated choices to forgive. I find that a lot more helpful. Whenever something reminds us of the wrongs, or the same things keep happening, we can choose all over again to hand it over to Jesus and leave it at the cross.

Chapter Seventeen

THE CHALLENGE OF REPENTANCE

In the early days, I assumed (maybe naively) that our workshop participants were all victims of Rwanda's terrible suffering and not perpetrators. Consequently, I didn't teach on personal repentance. But the local teams that we trained felt the need to do so, especially when perpetrators began to return from exile and prisoners started to be released. The prisons were so overcrowded that those who had confessed that what they did was wrong, were now being released into the community to continue their sentences in community service.

In my opinion, that is an excellent alternative. It's far better that they do something positive to rebuild their country and re-engage with their communities.

By this time Joseph Nyamutera had joined us as a teacher and wrote a chapter in our teaching book emphasising the true depth of Biblical repentance. This is a radical change of heart, accepting the consequences of one's actions and seeking to make amends wherever possible.

From this time on, during the Cross Session people who had never dealt with their sin were encouraged to put that on the cross as well as their pain. Even before that, we had started to hear different kinds of testimonies.

One pastor said, 'Until last night I was fooling everyone except myself and God. Even though I was a pastor, I was not a true Christian. When we came to put our pain on the cross, I was convicted that I had never put my sin there. I want to tell you that this morning I am standing here a new man.' The room burst into praise, singing a local song which had been popular during Rwanda's revival in the 1950s.

In another workshop, the Football (Soccer) World Cup happened to be showing on television the evening of the Cross Session. One of the participants was demanding insistently that a television be brought into the dining room so that they could all watch the match that evening and this was done. The next morning, he confessed to the group that he hadn't watched the match after all! He said, 'I laid down one burden at the cross yesterday afternoon and picked up another one. I began to be convicted of all the sin in my life. It was a terrible weight on my soul. So I went to my room and spent the whole evening confessing every sin I could think of and asking for God's forgiveness. This morning I feel so free!' God be praised.

Eliya, a Hutu, had been a Pentecostal evangelist before the genocide. He had learnt at his grandmother's knee to think badly of the Tutsi and when the genocide broke out, he joined the mob and killed many people. After some time he came under heavy conviction of sin. He kept seeing the faces of those he had killed and felt the Holy Spirit asking him, 'What did they do to deserve death?' He was in agony of spirit until he brokenly confessed his terrible sin and asked God for forgiveness. Peace began to flood his heart.

The first thing he did was to hand himself over to the authorities. After serving his sentence, he wondered how on earth he could try to make restitution for what he had done. He could never bring back those he had killed. He was a carpenter by trade and he decided he would offer to rebuild the doors and windows of damaged Tutsi homes and, in spite of extreme poverty, would never charge any Tutsi who required his carpentry service.

The first time I met Eliya, he said, 'Rhiannon, I don't deserve to be alive. Every day is a gift of God's grace and I mean to live every day for his glory.' He encountered Gaston in one of the workshops.

Eliya and me

Gaston and Eliya

He had killed 13 members of Gaston's wife's family. Amazingly Gaston was able to forgive after placing all his pain on the cross and they are now close friends who are highly respected in their community. Gaston was even Eliya's best man when he got married. They travel together to give their testimonies. Eliya is always careful to tell his story very truthfully and to take full responsibility for what he did.

A DIFFERENT KIND OF REPENTANCE

We discovered another major key that could unlock the hardest heart. On my first visit to Rwanda just twelve weeks post-genocide, I was invited to speak about Jesus, the healer of wounded hearts, at a meeting organised by World Vision, an international Christian relief organisation.

I had only been speaking for a few minutes when a lady stood up, her face contorted with anger. 'How dare you think you can come here to help us when you are the cause of all our problems in the first place!' she screamed.

I was shocked and confused – I was the cause? What could she possibly mean? Could she mean Europe? I turned to my translator for an explanation. He confirmed that Europe bore considerable responsibility for what had happened. 'Then please tell me,' I pleaded. 'They don't teach us these things in our country.'

He quickly summarised the fact that Germany and especially Belgium had used the 'divide and rule' policy there, turning one group against the other. They favoured the Tutsi group, until there was a revolution brewing and then switched allegiance to favour the Hutu.

THE CHALLENGE OF REPENTANCE

Belgium insisted on Rwandans having identity cards stating their group, similar to the ones they use back in Belgium between the Francophone part and the Flemish part. These identity cards were then used in the genocide against the Tutsi to determine who would live and who would die. When the genocide began, 12 Belgian soldiers working with the UN were killed, so a decision was made to pull out the UN. Only a few observers were left to monitor and film the genocide. Nothing was done to stop the killings.

I was horrified. Here I was in one of the worst affected places in Rwanda where the evidence of genocide was all around me. For me to discover that European politics had been the seed which eventually erupted as a genocide was unbearable. I started to weep, saying, 'I'm so sorry! I didn't know. That's terrible! That was so wrong!'

'OK, you can finish your talk,' she said and I had to try to compose myself to carry on with my message. At the end, when an invitation was given for anyone who would like to receive prayer, she was the first to come out. Through this incident, God impressed on me that the main reason He had brought me to Africa was to *ask* for forgiveness.

STANDING IN THE GAP

In my first workshop, as I prepared for how I should approach this, I struggled a bit. It was Germany and Belgium who had colonised Rwanda, not Wales. Did I have to apologise for something we hadn't done? I realised I had a choice.

I could excuse myself, or as a fellow-European coming from another colonising nation, I could identify with Germany and Belgium. What if no one from those countries ever comes here to apologise? I thought. Let me do it as a European. And I'm so glad I did. The principle of 'standing in the gap' on behalf of a nation or group has become one of the most powerful keys to bring healing.

I asked God to give me a gift of repentance and was going to start confessing Europe's unjust role in Rwanda's colonial history, when the Spirit alerted me that I needed to start much earlier than that. What about slavery? This had been a devastating wound to Africa which still has repercussions to the present day. And then, through stealing Africa's resources, we had raped this continent, and Europe became rich at Africa's expense.

But most of all, we had communicated a dehumanising message – that we were superior to them. This had robbed them of their dignity and value and was a deep wound to their spirit, which still affects them to this day.

During the genocide against the Tutsi we filmed the killings, doing nothing to stop the slaughter. We had abandoned them in their hour of greatest need. I asked the Lord to help me to list these things in detail. It was overwhelming.

As I expressed these things with tears, the first response was shock. They said they had never heard such things from a European before. But then the tears started to flow. They began to confess that they had hated us and started to ask my forgiveness for this. By now I have wept in the arms of hundreds of Africans as we embraced and wept together. It has been the means of incredible healing, giving them the opportunity to forgive and break their judgement that says, 'They are all the same.'

I have asked for forgiveness as a European not only in workshops, but also in schools, churches, public rallies, prisons, government prayer breakfasts… The response has been so powerful that I want to take every opportunity to bring further healing and release to people who have been wounded by us. But every time I do so, I need a fresh gift of repentance from God. It must never become mechanical.

I will never forget one meeting I attended with Joseph when I asked for the opportunity to apologise as a European. A headmaster stood up and said, 'Thank God I didn't die before today! I hated you people so much, I'm sure I would have gone straight to hell. What's more, I have taught my pupils to hate you. Can you ever forgive me?' We embraced and wept together. Then he pledged that he would return to his school and call all his pupils together. He would say it was time for all this hating to stop, because he had heard one European say 'Sorry'.

The most moving consequence was that people would say, 'If this stranger could come here and make herself vulnerable to us like this, can we not do this to one another? After all, even if they sowed the seeds, who was it that picked up the machetes?'

This would often lead into a spontaneous time of repentance which sometimes went on for several hours. This soon became a key principle in our teams. We called it 'Standing in the gap,' from Ezekiel 22:30, which says: *I looked for a man among them who would build up the wall and stand before me in the gap on behalf of the land so that I would not have to destroy it, but I found none.*' Anyone who wanted to be part of this ministry needed to be willing to 'stand in the gap' on behalf of their group.

2 Corinthians 10:4 speaks of unconventional weapons that can bring down spiritual strongholds. Our experience is that this must be one of them, demolishing strongholds of hatred and bitterness. Thousands of people in Rwanda will confess today that they owe their healing to people who were willing to stand in the gap. Often this would prepare their hearts for the time when they would be confronted with the real perpetrator.

I want to honour my Rwandan brother Joseph. Probably what impacted him the most during his first workshop was experiencing Anastase, Kristine and myself 'standing in the gap.' As a Hutu he was weighed down with the guilt of what his group had done and he felt great shame for being a Hutu. He didn't know how to cope with that. After understanding the principle of 'standing in the gap' he realised what he could do to help his nation heal. He has asked for forgiveness as a Hutu hundreds, if not thousands of times by now and always at great emotional cost. But the fruit has been wonderful.

Jacqueline, a Tutsi growing up in exile in Uganda, had always hated Hutu. When she heard news of the genocide in Rwanda, her hatred knew no bounds. She moved to live in Rwanda after the genocide had ended and became a pastor, but would not allow any Hutu into her church.

She attended a workshop and was horrified to see Joseph as a Hutu doing some of the teaching. But after Joseph asked forgiveness as a Hutu, her heart was changed. She ran out of the room to get a new piece of material she had bought to make a

THE CHALLENGE OF REPENTANCE

skirt and gave it to Joseph. 'Use this as a doormat,' she said, 'and every time you wipe your feet on it, you can remember there is a Tutsi who has forgiven.'

The next day as the team were leaving, she ran after the car, begging Joseph to allow her to become his daughter. She has now become a much loved member of his family, staying in their home many times and has now married a Hutu. We could tell many such stories of shocking forgiveness that have taken place after someone has 'stood in the gap'.

When we teach this topic, we first show the participants this drawing that was done in Rwanda, asking them what they see in it. This helps to lead into the teaching.

What do you see when you look at this picture?

Apparently, the concept of confessing and repenting on behalf of your group is a contentious issue among theologians –

International community asking forgiveness in Rwanda, July 2009

Western ones, that is. We in the West are so individualistic, thinking only of me and God, but other cultures understand this principle very well.

Leviticus 26:40 teaches the need of not only confessing our own sins but also those of our fathers. Of course, this does not in any way absolve the guilt of the past. Only God can deal with that. While the theologians are debating, we seek to continue to faithfully obey what God has shown us. Jesus said we would know the tree by its fruit. And the fruit is undeniable not only in Africa but in many parts of the world by now. Along with the Cross Session, it is probably the most effective way of seeing healing and reconciliation take place. It has become a lifestyle. (For more understanding about this topic, see our online teaching book *Healing Hearts, Transforming Nations*, which is freely downloadable on the website: www.HHTNglobal.org.)

THE CHALLENGE OF REPENTANCE

MAKING IT A LIFESTYLE

I have now had the privilege of 'standing in the gap' in many parts of the world. It is now a strong calling on my life, especially in countries that we British colonised. Our superior, dominating, and arrogant attitude has wounded so many. And, uninvited, we have forced our culture, language and way of doing things on other nationalities wherever we went. It broke my heart when someone in Kenya said to me, 'You didn't only colonise our countries. You colonised our *minds*.'

I was on holiday in Trinidad a few years ago, staying with friends who had previously been members of my church. On my arrival, they said they hoped I didn't mind, but they had arranged for me to be interviewed on a Christian radio programme.

I agreed and was questioned about our work of reconciliation. It was a live programme and before the programme ended, I said there was something important I wanted to do. I proceeded to ask forgiveness as a British citizen for our role in the evil slave trade and for our unjust colonial rule there.

The interviewer, a slave descendant, was completely taken aback and didn't know what to do. 'Oh my goodness… Oh my goodness…' she said, and started to weep. People then started phoning in, thanking me for my message of repentance and saying things like, 'For the first time I feel free'. 'I forgive you on behalf of my grandparents.' I was then asked to do this on television and the response was amazing. It was worth going all the way to Trinidad to experience that.

I have also had to ask forgiveness as a doctor. In a workshop in Ukraine, a man told us that 35 years previously his baby son had been taken to a hospital for immunisation and was given an injection of chemotherapy by mistake, which killed him. When I heard this, I knew there was something I had to do and went to kneel at his feet. An American nurse who was present also joined me and we confessed the fallibility of the medical profession, expressing great sorrow for this terrible injustice. He broke down in tears, saying that this was the first time he had heard an apology. He said that for the first time in 35 years, he could now let this go and feel his heart being healed. Thank You, Jesus!

Chapter Eighteen

INVITATION TO SOUTH AFRICA

By now, other countries were hearing about the blessing in Rwanda and doors were opening for us to share what we had learnt the hard way.

The next country where the workshop was conducted was South Africa and I began to work there in 1996. Michael Cassidy and his team from African Enterprise had come from South Africa to conduct a mission in Rwanda in 1995. I had told them then that I had a burden for South Africa and would like to conduct our HWEC workshop there. Apartheid had been dismantled structurally in 1994, but it was still there in many hearts. This location turned out to be a lot harder than Rwanda.

A Black leader said to me, 'No one White has anything to say to us', while a White (English) lady said that they were now the wounded ones. The Afrikaners were understandably very defensive, believing the whole world would be condemning them for apartheid.

I prayed for some link with the various people groups. I was excited to discover that Zulu (and some of the other Black languages) had a sound that was very similar to our Welsh 'LL' (though written 'HL').

With the first Zulu audience, I told them this and pronounced for them Hluhluwe, the name of a nearby safari game park. They were amazed. I said that very few languages had that sound, so we Welsh must be their long-long lost cousins who had migrated north and the cold weather had turned our skins pale. They laughed and laughed, and I knew I had found a way into their hearts.

But would I ever find a link with the Afrikaners? Again God was faithful. I discovered that, before the Boer War, they were punished by the English for speaking Afrikaans in school and had to wear a wooden board around their necks. So I told them the story of the 'Welsh Not' (described in Chapter 4) and they warmed immediately. 'So you understand us!' they exclaimed.

This was further cemented when, in repentance, I washed the feet of Afrikaner men whose grandmothers had been in the concentration camps that the British had installed during the Boer War, where mothers and children were starved to death. They wept openly, saying they had never heard such an apology before. (At least one Welsh regiment was involved in the Boer War, and in the battles against the Zulu.)

One of the things I felt strongly when starting to work in South Africa was that, as in Rwanda, it would be helpful to stay in the homes of the different ethnic groups. That would be the way to hear their hearts and, in such a divided country, it would be so important to hear everyone's perspective. Staying in people's homes would give me a good understanding and equip me better to help, than just staying in a hotel would do. So I was delighted as opportunities arose for me to stay in various homes. And each visit was an interesting and valuable educational experience.

BLACK TOWNSHIP

I really wanted to stay in a Black township, so was happy when a friend in the HWEC workshop agreed that I could stay overnight with him and his wife in Katlehong, Johannesburg. The home was small and it was clear that it would be very hot in summer and very cold in winter. They kept apologising for the basic conditions, but it was such a joy having rich fellowship with them. 'We must take you to visit some of our neighbours.' they said. 'They will be so thrilled that you are staying in our township.'

One elderly lady asked someone to pinch her. 'Am I really awake, or is this a dream?' she asked. 'Can it possibly be true that a White person is visiting me in my poor home?'

Later I was asked why I hadn't been afraid to stay in the township. In fact, the neighbouring community there was so warm and welcoming, that it was the place I felt the most safe in all my visits to South Africa. My friends told me the community were so grateful for the visit that they would protect me with their lives.

I had the joy of staying with another HWEC workshop participant and his wife in a poorer township in KwaZulu Natal. They only had one bedroom which was behind a partition with the living room / kitchen. They insisted on my sleeping in their bed while they shared the sofa. They were so thrilled at my visit that he arranged a special meeting to welcome me in the small church which he was pastoring. I was overwhelmed at the love and welcome I received, and was moved to tears when they took up an offering for me. They apologised it was so little because they were poor, but said it would be enough to buy me a bottle of Coke.

Since then I have received a warm welcome on several occasions in the home of a pastor in Vosloorus, Johannesburg, who became part of the team. They accepted me as one of the family.

COLOURED (MIXED RACE) COMMUNITY

Again, it was a joy to stay in a Coloured community both in Benoni and Heidelberg in Gauteng and in Jeffrey's Bay in the Cape.

'Coloured' was a legally defined racial classification given to brown, multi-racial people during apartheid. Most were from mixed ancestry but also included the Khoisan people. During apartheid, everyone had to marry within their own grouping, so the Coloured people, in effect, became their own ethnic group with their own culture. Some find the name offensive and prefer to be known as the 'so-called Coloured', but for many their identity as a group is still acceptable.

Although they are the people group who feel the most rejected in South Africa (see the later section on the Thief Session), I found that they had an amazing gift of humour. This is the way they coped with their pain. They were a very lively group and it was great fun to be with them.

AN AFRIKANER HOUSEHOLD IN POTCHEFSTROOM

This was a very different experience. A friend invited me to stay in her parents' home, but warned me that their views were very different from her own. As I entered the house, her father greeted me, asking where I was from. When I told him it was Britain, he said, 'You're so lucky! You're not surrounded by b… Blacks like we are!' I was dumbfounded.

How should I respond? I decided the best thing at that point was to say nothing. I was just on the point of being welcomed as a guest in their home. I experienced great hospitality there, but learnt a lot too. It was useful to hear their hearts.

Since then I have stayed in very different Afrikaner homes – people whom God has raised up to be part of the healing and reconciliation team. In one of these homes, I began to understand more of the very limited information they had been given during apartheid. Some of their reactions were due to ignorance and I needed to be patient.

We watched the DVD 'Sarafina' with Whoopi Goldberg, based on the massacre of the Black children in Soweto in 1976 during a schools' uprising against apartheid. I had just bought this and was eager to see it. The reaction of my hosts shocked me.

They were so angry. 'This is all lies!' they exclaimed. 'It's all Black propaganda. Our police would *never* have killed children!' I couldn't convince them it was true and had been reported on our news at home.

Soon afterwards, they approached a friend who was in the police force, asking for confirmation that this had never happened. They were heartbroken to discover that it had actually happened. They are now very quick to repent on behalf of the apartheid government, especially as they discover more of the truth. This showed me that I should not be quick to judge, but as it says in James 1:19, we should be *'slow to speak and quick to listen'.*

AN INDIAN HOME IN DURBAN

South Africa has the highest number of Indians outside India. We British brought them over to work the sugarcane plantations, promising they would soon be so rich they could return to India to help their families. That was not true – they were little more than slaves and the vast majority were never able to return.

Knowing this, it was particularly meaningful for me to be able to share an Indian home for a while and be able to hear the Indian perspective. They received me so lovingly and treated me as one of their family, showering hospitality on me. I must admit there were times when I longed for *anything* that wasn't curried…

ENGLISH HOMES

I had wonderful hospitality in a range of English homes, but I always tried to get to know the house servants wherever I stayed in Africa.

Once, when travelling with my friend and assistant Kristine, staying in the home of a well-to-do White family, we tried to get to know the Black housemaid. We asked if we could visit her in the servant quarters she occupied at the back of the family home and share a meal with her. 'But I only eat pap (cornmeal).' she protested. 'That's fine,' we said, 'we'll come and eat pap with you.'

She couldn't believe her ears. 'You want to come to eat pap with me in my poor house?' She took some persuading, but nervously agreed. There was a huge disparity between the furnishings in the two houses. We had a special evening with her, finding out about her family and interests. Not long afterwards, it was heart-breaking to hear she had been killed in a road accident.

Chapter Nineteen

NEW CREATIVE IDEAS IN SOUTH AFRICA

It became clear that some things had to be modified for the very different situation in South Africa. How could I emphasise the importance of unity in diversity? Here, unlike in Rwanda where they sought uniformity, it was going to be important to honour the different ethnic groups and celebrate their diversity while at the same time experiencing unity. I had the sudden thought of starting the workshop by exploring the relationships between the Trinity – Father, Son and Holy Spirit.

THE MEANING OF EVERYTHING

Why did it take me so long for me to learn this – that life is all about relationships? It's all so simple. The Godhead is an amazing loving, united relationship and we were created for loving, united relationships. They don't *have* love, they *are* love and that's very different – and mind-blowing. Seemingly, the Godhead, who had experienced perfect love and unity for all eternity, agreed that what they had between them was too good to keep to themselves. So they decided, 'Let us make man in our image.'

It has been a long journey of revelation for me, a journey out of a legalistic view of God with a list of requirements for humanity and a journey into the loving heart of the Godhead. I'm still discovering more and I love what I'm finding. Why do we complicate things? It doesn't get more complicated the more understanding I receive, but more simple. We were created to share the life of the Trinity. We were designed for glorious living! Every aspect of our life was meant to be full of glory. How far we have fallen short of this.

I don't remember the first time I spontaneously decided to invite three people to join hands to form a circle to symbolise the Trinity. 'Let's explore what's happening between these Three,' I suggested. 'How do they relate to one another? Describe to me the quality of this relationship.' We discovered that, though the Three were distinct, they were perfectly united. Difference had not been a problem throughout eternity.

There had never been even one negative thought about each other. There was no competition, no jealousy, no one feeling threatened, no domination. Rather there was such an enjoyment of each other, such a celebration of their loving unity, each complementing the others. Above all else, there was no selfishness – the opposite of love and therefore the root of all sinfulness and division. We tried to imagine what it would be like to be part of such a relationship.

The next question was, 'So why did they create us? Why didn't they carry on loving each other for ever?' We concluded that love always seeks someone to love. They wanted to share with us the amazing loving unity they had been experiencing throughout eternity. We then opened up the circle, asking, 'If you would like to experience this amazing relationship of love and unity, come and join the circle.' I explained that this is the goal we are aiming for – to rediscover God's original plan – a quest that will keep us engaged for the rest of our lives. This is the goal for all our relationships – to experience loving unity with the Trinity and with one another.

Soon I came to believe that this was the most effective way to start the workshop. If we got this right, everything else would follow. By now, I have done this so many times in so many countries and I always love these sessions.

Sometimes people eagerly come to join the circle; for others there's a hesitation. But usually in the end, everyone comes. It's great to see people becoming excited about the reason they were created. We leave one part of the circle open, because with God there's always room for more. As we were *all* created in Their image, there is no basis for racism or ethnic superiority. There is only one human race. We were created for community, to live as a loving united family.

It's only recently that I've realised that, without the Trinity, we could never say that God is love, because love requires relationship. The loving unity between the three Persons of the Trinity is totally foundational to our understanding of life. It's all about love. This really is the meaning of everything.

Next, it was important to explore whether diversity was a curse or a blessing. Was it God's plan that we should be different people groups? When a country has suffered conflict and division, often the conclusion is that it's a curse, that it wasn't God's plan. The biblical story of the tower of Babel seems to confirm their view. But there are always some who believe that God intended diversity to be a blessing.

We then confirm this from what we know of God – that He loves diversity. We only have to look at creation to see that. As already pointed out in chapter 4, Acts 17:26 tells that, '*From one man He made every nation (= ethne) of men.*' Diversity was definitely His idea. And if we all came from one man, then we are all the same underneath our different skins. I emphasised what a blessing black skin is in strong sunlight. It is God's wisdom for protection. We pale-skinned people have to wear sunscreen cream or we get burnt and may develop skin cancer. To suggest that people of different skin colour had a different value was senseless and a misunderstanding of God's wisdom.

On hearing this, one Zulu lady cried out, 'Is that right? We're all the same underneath? Then I'm already healed! I can go home happily now.' I encouraged her not to go home yet as there were a lot more blessings in store.

Remembering South Africa's diamond mines, I asked if someone could come out and draw us a diamond and we explored together why a diamond is so much more valuable than a pane of glass. We concluded it was all the various facets or faces of the diamond that made it so different, whereas a pane of glass has only one face. Each facet reflects the light in a unique way, creating the amazing beauty of a diamond. It is also much stronger than glass and can even be used to cut through metal. I suggested that we were all designed by God to form a huge, magnificent diamond, each people group reflecting God's glory in some unique way.

In later workshops, we would write the names of the various people groups into the facets. For Szabina, a Roma gypsy from Hungary, seeing her people group as one of the facets in that diamond was life-transforming, as she was able to accept for the first time that the Roma also were part of God's beautiful creation, loved and honoured by Him. Szabina later was to become a valued member of the international teaching team.

Another short impromptu drama helped to drive the point home that diversity was always meant to be a blessing. I asked a Black lady to stand at the front on the opposite side of the room. I then played out two possible scenarios. In the first, I was excited at meeting someone different, eager to get to know her, to learn her culture and the wisdom of her people. We ended up embracing each other. Then I said, 'Let's see what usually happens.' This time I stopped when I saw her, feeling threatened and expressing much prejudice. I said there was no way we could share the same land, so I staked my claim on it forcibly. I decided to build a wall to safeguard my own interests, but then discovered that was not enough. I also needed a weapon.

At this point I asked the participants how they were feeling during the two dramas, then moving on to how God feels about those scenarios. The message hit home. This little drama has now become a significant part of the start of the HWEC workshop. Unless we can grasp that God greatly values our diversity and gives us all equal value, there will be no true reconciliation.

EXPANDING THE CONCEPT OF THE THIEF

Other aspects of the workshop were also modified, including the teaching on the Thief. Before our wounds could be healed, we needed to identify what they were.

In Rwanda, for the sake of political correctness, we had considered what Satan the Thief (John 10:10) had stolen from the whole country. It became clear that here in South Africa each group would need to own their individual losses. I apologised that we would need to go back to apartheid for a short while, and asked people to go into their own ethnic groups, taking a flip chart and pen. They were asked to list both their losses and their false beliefs. This led to much lively discussion within the groups as they composed their lists.

Having a feedback time was crucial so that each group could be listened to with respect, accepting that everyone's pain was valid. It was also important for people to listen to the pain of other groups, as it was all too easy to believe that they were the only true losers. Often it was the first time for the groups to really hear the experiences of the other groups. The false beliefs were heartbreaking:

'The Whites are the blessed and we are the cursed.'

'God is the God of the Whites.'

'We Coloured (mixed-race) people are the garbage of the nation, the product of adultery, we are even an embarrassment to God.'

'We Whites were created to be superior.'

The people of colour were surprised to hear the White people say that they had also been robbed – of humility, of the opportunity to enjoy the culture of other groups, of hearing truth on the media, as well as painful experiences pre-dating apartheid. It became clear that, from God's perspective, there were no winners and realising this was part of the healing.

Finally these lists were all nailed to the cross and it was a revelation to many that Jesus had also taken the pain of their ethnic groups. Because it was so important to end this session on a positive note, we would focus on the hope of restoration. Jesus had bought back on the cross all that the enemy had stolen from them and was offering them life in all its fullness. I'll never forget in one workshop, a group of young people from the Coloured group saying they wanted to sing a short song, written by Richard Black, after sharing their losses:

> *I went to the enemy's camp*
> *and I took back what he stole from me*

It was encouraging to hear that they did not want to be resigned to their losses, but with God's help would seek to take them back and rise above them. That became a powerful song to sing at the end of the Thief session.

After we had sung it in another workshop in Durban, a White pastor said in tears to the other nationalities, 'I've been robbed of you and I want you back.' He suggested we stand in a circle and sing it again. This time we should cross over to someone we had not been able to relate to previously and 'take them back'. What a wonderful time that was. At one juncture, I noticed a Black Pentecostal pastor dancing with a White Catholic nun!

THE HOLY NATION ROBE

The Holy Nation teaching became particularly important in South Africa, as it emphasises the equal value of each people group. An Indian lady in Durban made me a beautiful purple royal robe with a gold trimming, around the bottom of which the flags of many nations were later sewn. She also made me a waistcoat to which I later attached a big Welsh flag. I now use this in a small drama where I start by wearing the waistcoat, explaining how my natural identity was a wounded one. The more it was attacked and despised, the more it became an idol, close to my heart.

I tell the story of my encounter with the Holy Spirit when I first realised my citizenship in the Holy Nation. Someone holds up the beautiful robe for me and I ask the audience which I should wear. It's amazing to me that, even in the middle of civil war, they have pointed to the robe, saying, 'Go for that one. It's much better!' 'But this is my tribe,' I say. 'It's my identity.' 'No, take the other one!' they cry, and applaud when I remove my waistcoat and put on the robe.

Showing my Welsh waistcoat in a sensitive country

God does not ask us to lay anything down without

offering us a better alternative. I point out that, wearing this robe, I no longer need to walk around as an angry, wounded person, because my Welsh flag is also at the bottom of this robe. It's no longer an idol close to my heart but takes its place among all the other flags. In the Holy Nation we have equal value and can honour one another, celebrating the diversity. At last God's original intention can begin to be realised.

Wearing the Holy Nation Robe

In one workshop in Durban, a Coloured man asked me, 'So what flag can I put on my robe?' When I asked his background, he said his forefathers were both Afrikaner and Zulu. 'So you are *doubly* blessed.' I said. 'You have two flags you can put on your robe and you can embrace the cultural gifts of both ethnic groups.' As people left at the end of the workshop, he came to give me a hug, thanking me for his *two* flags.

Since then I have found the wearing of the robe to be particularly effective for people struggling with their identity. For example, in more than one workshop, a German person has spoken of the shame of their nation's history. Each time I have called them to the front and asked them to don the robe. Germany's flag is also there and we pray with them to honour them, and welcome them as full citizens of the Holy Nation. This is where the redemptive gifts of Germany can be rediscovered as God had always intended: to be used for the glory of God and the extension of His Kingdom.

After pointing this out in another workshop, a young German woman called Anne who had rejected her nationality, was able to wear the robe and sing the German anthem for the first time.

In another HWEC workshop, Nicole, the daughter of missionaries of different nationalities, shared that she had been brought up in yet another country and confessed she didn't really have any place she could call 'home'. Being called forward to wear the Holy Nation robe brought her so much joy. Here she was a full citizen.

In a workshop in Ukraine, Margarita shared that she didn't know who she really was or where she belonged. Her father was Polish, a country she loved passionately, but whose language she couldn't speak, whilst so many other Polish children at school were fluent. Her mother's family were originally Norwegian; she was born in England and is now married to a Welshman and lives in Wales.

We called her to come and put on the robe, stating that she belonged as a full citizen in the Holy Nation. She was moved to tears and wore the robe for the rest of the morning. She told us later that this had been a very healing experience for her and she didn't want to take it off.

Even in Rwanda, where it would not be politically correct to honour the Hutu, the Tutsi and the Twa as separate groups, the Holy Nation teaching was very meaningful. In the early days of the ministry there, one lady jumped up after I testified of the way the Holy Nation concept had become life transforming for me. 'I knew it.' she cried. 'God had revealed this to me a long time ago but the recent experiences had robbed me of it. I'm taking it back into my heart today.'

Appreciating the Holy Nation became a great equaliser in Rwanda, where the Tutsi could lay down their victim identity and the Hutu their oppressor identity. It gave both groups a right to work together in the task of healing the nation.

CELEBRATING UNITY IN DIVERSITY

In Rwanda, the workshop would end with the time of repentance, but I felt it was important to end the workshop in South Africa with a celebration of unity in diversity as fellow-citizens in the Holy Nation. But what would be the best way of doing that?

The idea came of having a special meal, a modification of the one we used to have in the Operation Mobilisation (OM) courses in North Wales. It was called The King's Table. There would be room for everyone to participate at this Table and everyone would be welcome. We would all approach it as equals and would affirm, honour and bless one another. Kristine and I got excited about that and decided to secretly prepare as beautiful and majestic a table as possible, abundantly laden with good things.

We also had the idea of making crowns out of gold or coloured card, but not to put on our own heads. They were to be placed on the head of someone from a different ethnic group, saying, 'Welcome to the King's Table, fellow-citizen in the Holy Nation!' As different ethnic groups, we would serve each other.

Crowns

We tried this idea and many were overwhelmed as they entered and saw the magnificent Table to which they were all invited on an equal basis. It was such a surprise. The joy was wonderful to behold. After sharing the meal together, we took time to affirm each group, beginning with the ones who had felt the most despised.

The King's Table

A representative of each group was given the Holy Nation robe to wear. We first asked, 'What do you appreciate about this group? What is the treasure God has put into them?' Earlier in the workshop we always identify the prejudices underlying every ethnic conflict because we realise how destructive these prejudices are. Now we were publicly affirming one another, coming in the opposite spirit.

We heard things like:

'You Coloured people have a great sense of humour and you are ideally placed to be bridge-builders, bringing White and Black together.'

'You Black people know how to persevere in difficult times and to go through suffering and still come out singing and dancing.'

'You Indians place much value on family ties, and you are very hospitable.'

'You Afrikaners know how to be strong leaders. And you're very good at rugby.'

'You English people are such good organisers and time-keepers.'

Then we asked, 'How would you like to see these people blessed?' The Bible puts a lot of emphasis on the power of blessing. The power of life and death is in the tongue (Proverbs 18:21). It can bring healing or pierce the heart (Proverbs 12:18). It can be a tree of life or it can crush the spirit (Proverbs 15:4). Pronouncing blessings in the name of the Lord was one of the functions of the priesthood (Deuteronomy 10:8). God is calling His people to be those who pronounce blessings, not judgments.

It was something the Hebrew people took very seriously and was an integral part of their culture. Kings blessed their subjects, fathers blessed their children. Seemingly, people would pronounce blessings on each other as they met in the market place. Jesus took it further and told us even to bless our enemies. (Luke 6:28).

Words of blessing carried great power and withholding a blessing was experienced as a tragedy, as when Jacob deceived his father Isaac into giving him the blessing intended for Esau, the eldest son (Genesis 27).

Today, many of us like Esau are crying out in our hearts, 'Is there no blessing left for me?' (Genesis 27:36). Whole people groups can be wondering, 'Do you only have one blessing, my Father? Bless me too, my Father!' (Genesis 27:38). It is heartbreaking if you believe that there is only limited blessing available and it doesn't include your group.

After a wonderful time of blessing each other, we ended by asking each group for a demonstration of their culture and this led into a joyful time of singing and dancing. It really was a time of celebration.

At first, all the songs used in the workshop were English language songs. When I asked if they knew any Zulu songs, I was met with a shocked, blank stare. So I need to learn a Zulu song, I thought, and an Afrikaner one and maybe a Sotho one. I also felt I had to quickly learn the South African national anthem. This was a challenge that I loved and soon I was able to start singing a short song in other South African languages. The response was immediate – such joy as the relevant group joined in. Soon the teams that were trained were using songs in all the major South African languages.

Reconciliation in South Africa

But there was one group that made me feel sad. The Indians in South Africa had seemingly lost their cultural heritage when they became Christians, having been told that Asian culture was evil. The truth is that there is good and bad in *every* culture. Revelation 21:26 says that the glory and honour of all the nations (=*ethnos*) will be brought into the new Jerusalem. So we need to embrace everything that's good in our cultures and that can be used for God's glory. But verse 27 says that nothing impure will enter in, so we must renounce everything that's not in line with the values of God's Kingdom, and leave it at the cross.

I prayed for God's help and was overjoyed when someone told me of an album called Asia Worships, which had been made by Kensington Temple, a multi-cultural church in London. I managed to find one of these and it was beautiful.

In the next workshop in South Africa, I played the first song, 'Peace comes to you in Jesus' name'. This was sung in both English and Hindi, with Indian tunes and instrumentation. When I played it, the Indians started to weep. 'This is you,' I said, 'and if we don't hear your voice, something is missing in the expression of the Holy Nation in South Africa.' I heard later that they had purchased this album and were now teaching these Hindi worship songs in their churches in Durban. That was a joy to hear.

This first King's Table was such a success that we decided always to end the workshop in this way. I never cease to marvel at the change in atmosphere between the beginning and end of the workshop.

One very articulate, well informed Xhosa young lady had been very angry at the beginning, saying to the Afrikaners, 'Go back to where you belong. We don't want you here!' After the Cross Session, she remarked the next morning, 'I don't know what happened to me at the cross last night, but this morning, I love you all!' And amazingly, at the King's Table, she pleaded with the Afrikaners not to leave because they could work together to transform South Africa.

Often the Afrikaners were the last to be called forward, thinking that no one was going to want to affirm and bless them because apartheid originated from them. But by that stage of the workshop, the participants were so healed that they affirmed and blessed the Afrikaners more than anyone.

When I started to work in other countries, it was clear that the King's Table would always be a wonderful way to end the workshop. Some Tables looked quite barren in comparison with the South African one, especially the one in DR Congo in the middle of a civil war, but they still loved it. By now, there have been so many amazing experiences at the King's Table.

It is wonderful to hear groups that had previously not honoured, even hated one another now affirming one another and pronouncing blessing on one another:

'May your people have plenty to eat!'

'May your children have good education and good health care!'

'May your country / tribe know lasting peace!'

Ukrainians at a workshop near the frontline of battle, who had come to the workshop hating Russians, were now pronouncing blessings on them! Only God can work such miracles.

For me, this time of blessing is usually the highlight of the whole workshop and we also believe that this is a powerful effect for good in the spiritual realm.

Chapter Twenty

THE MESSAGE SPREADS TO CONGO

When the border between Rwanda and the Democratic Republic of Congo was suddenly closed, I was so relieved. This was Easter 2004 and I was scheduled to visit Bunia, in Ituri, northeastern DR Congo where civil war had been raging for years.

I was very nervous. 'The UN are in Bunia,' they said. 'It's the only place where it's safe for you to come.' But I wasn't convinced, especially as I would have to cross the border from Rwanda into Goma and had been warned that Goma airport could be a nightmare.

The first invitation had come early in 2002, after a Medair relief worker who had been debriefed in Le Rucher, Geneva, had taken the workshop teaching book to Nyankunde hospital. (Older readers may be interested to know that's where the missionary Helen Roseveare had worked.)

Daniel Mas Kasereka, who had been the hospital accountant, had contacted me, saying he had read the book. He was convinced that this was the ministry they needed there and invited me to come to conduct a workshop for the staff of this Christian hospital. So I had planned to visit in November 2002, taking a Hutu and Tutsi from Rwanda with me as a living demonstration of what God could do.

But in September 2002, Nyankunde hospital had been attacked and largely destroyed and many people in the region were killed. I didn't know if Daniel was still alive. I heard nothing until December 2002. Daniel had taken refuge in Nairobi and asked if a new copy of the teaching book could be sent to him there. Reading that book transformed his thinking, enabling him to forgive those who tried to kill him.

He was convinced that he should return to DR Congo to take the message to his fellow-countrymen. Early in 2004, I heard from him again, saying that the hospital staff had been scattered over the region, but in every place had started a prayer group. They were now ready for the workshop.

Putting flowers into the ashes in DR Congo

To my consternation, the border suddenly opened again, giving me no excuse for not going. Thankfully, a pastor in Goma, who had been through our workshop in northern Rwanda, volunteered to come with me to make sure I was safe. We flew into Bunia the week after Easter 2004 and held the first workshop in DR Congo, where 54 Christian leaders had assembled together to hear our message.

From the start I could see that these people were serious about becoming peacemakers in their troubled land. They were so responsive, even starting to repent on day 2 though that was meant to be the message of day 3! At the end they were convinced. 'With this message, we can stop this war,' they exclaimed. 'Money or no money, we will do it.'

THE TRIP TO BENI

Following the destruction of Nyankunde, many people from the tribes of that whole region of Ituri had walked south for many dangerous days through the jungle to reach Beni, a town in North Kivu, the next state. So there was a sizeable population of displaced people there. The participants of that first workshop in Bunia said, 'Now that we are healed, we must go down to Beni to be reconciled with those people!'

A workshop was arranged there for my next visit – one that I will never forget. I watched as people piled into the back of a big truck in Bunia for the 11-hour journey south through the jungle. They were singing, carrying a picture of a cross. I was choked up, wondering if they would arrive alive, as the war was still continuing and there were many militia roadblocks on the way. I wanted to travel with them, but they refused. 'Your white face will make it more dangerous for us,' they explained, 'because they will think there's money available. You need to fly down there.' Reluctantly I had to agree.

What jubilation there was when the truck rolled in safely. And what a welcome they were given by the displaced people. There were over 100 in that workshop, probably the biggest one I have conducted, and the tearful repentance and reconciliation at the end were unforgettable.

I was puzzled when they began to pick up books, bags, even chairs, putting them on their heads, singing and marching around the room. I discovered they were singing that they were leaving the place of slavery and were on their way to Canaan, the Promised Land. Another song was accompanied by salutes – to their new Commander in Chief, King Jesus!

At the King's Table, which was a meagre affair, they blessed one another saying things like, 'May God give you many more children to replace the ones our tribe killed' and 'May God give you good grazing land for your cattle', amazing but appropriate, considering much of the war was about land. Sometime during the evening, the generator petered out (there was no electricity in Beni at that time) and we were plunged into darkness. Undaunted, they drove a couple of Land Rovers up to the doors with full headlights on.

I had been accommodated in a Protestant guesthouse (seemingly the only safe place for a foreigner), and as we approached 10 pm, because of the curfew, they ushered me out to be taken there. The next morning, I heard that the King's Table celebration had continued the whole night. Sometime in the early hours of the morning, they had knelt together, committing themselves to be peacemakers in DR Congo.

That small beginning led to an amazing work of healing and reconciliation in the whole region. In the early days of the ministry there, they walked for days to reach various communities, or travelled in the back of trucks for hours. But soon the word got out that wherever this team went, roadblocks were dismantled and enemies became friends.

A Christian relief organisation approached them, saying how impressed they were with the results of their ministry and offering to support them financially. This was very encouraging news, until they added that, as some of their funding came from government, they would have to omit anything that could be offensive. 'So please leave out the cross.' I was so proud of them when I heard that they had smiled, saying, 'Thank you. You can keep your money and we will keep the cross.' There was no way they were going to attempt to run this workshop without the cross!

Happily, other funding became available. In addition, Missionary Aviation Fellowship (MAF) pledged to fly them anywhere for free, as they could see the fruit of their work.

Later, Daniel, who had not grown up in a Christian home, told me that his mother had gone to a witchdoctor when she was expecting him, seeking an abortion. The witchdoctor said, 'I cannot abort this one, because he is going to become a man of God.' Daniel's early years of wild living are ones that he now deeply regrets. At a later age he became a believer and I certainly confirm that he is now a mighty man of God. He leads the team in DR Congo and is one of the most godly people I know.

Workshops always ended in great joy, participants having experienced deep reconciliation. At the end of one workshop, they left the King's Table together and piled into the back of a truck, still wearing their crowns, and drove through the town singing loudly. The militia in that area were known by their headdress and, sure enough, they were stopped by the police asking their identity. 'We belong to the Holy Nation,' they exclaimed.

Daniel

Standing in the gap as a Welsh person was also important there. Before being allowed to conduct the first workshop, I had to present myself before the local government. In such a tense and dangerous time, they wanted to know who I was and what I would be doing. After I explained the nature of the HWEC workshop, I added that I was also aware of the need for reconciliation with Europe.

Coming from Wales, where Henry Morton Stanley had been born, I wanted to ask forgiveness for all the atrocities committed under his leadership. He had been King Leopold's righthand man when Congo was colonised by Belgium and Stanley was the one who carried out his deadly policies. King Leopold himself had never gone there. Hearing this, the officials readily gave me permission.

GODLESS CHIEFS ARE INVITED TO JOIN THE TRINITY CIRCLE

I remember conducting this workshop for city chiefs in Bunia. The atmosphere in the room was tense. It was the first time the two sides had sat together since the start of the war. 'When are we going to have a debate?' asked one of the chiefs. 'We want to know whose fault this war is.' Daniel remarked that there wouldn't be any debate. 'No debate? Then why are we here?' he demanded angrily. Daniel asked them to stay calm because we were going to start somewhere very different. We were going to start by thinking about the time before the world had even been created. We then did the Trinity circle.

When I asked who would like to join the circle, no one moved. So I waited. Eventually, one chief got up, then another, then another… In the end, the whole room had joined the circle. The chief who had objected at the beginning asked, 'Is this why we were created? And look what we've done!' I explained that the goal of reconciliation is not achieved when we've stopped killing each other but rather when we discover God's original plan for us. This workshop would help us begin the journey back towards what God intended. Did they want to stay? The unanimous decision was 'Yes!'

LINGUISTIC BENEFITS

I loved the sound of their Swahili language. Having grown up in a minority linguistic and cultural ethnic group, I was particularly interested in language and culture. Swahili, like Welsh, is phonetic, so I would read it as if it were Welsh. 'You know our language!' they cried excitedly. 'No I don't, but I would like to.' I responded. 'But you sound as if you really know it!' they said. Knowing Welsh has helped me with many phonetic languages, enabling me to pronounce their words correctly.

Knowing how precious it is to us whenever other language groups try to learn some Welsh, I always like to learn a few phrases in every country that I go to. This helps a heart connection to develop quickly.

(I don't always get it right. In Rwanda, I learnt how to say 'love, peace and joy', in their language. The problem is that the word for joy and the word for beans are very similar. I wondered why people started laughing, when I proudly announced that Jesus had come to give us 'love, peace and…beans!')

IMPACTING THE REGIONAL CHIEFS

Fairly early on in the ministry, two Regional Chiefs on opposites sides of the conflict in Ituri met in a workshop and were reconciled. They then approached the team asking them if they would conduct the workshop for all the Regional Chiefs in Ituri province. 'This can stop the war,' they said. 'So we will call them together, if you will take them to the cross, just like you took us. Give them the same message – don't change anything.' These Chiefs are powerful people, much more influential than government officials.

By this time, the team's faith was growing as they had seen God at work so much, so they agreed. But first they wanted to organise a continual chain of prayer day and night for three months, as the victory had to be won in prayer first.

Daniel and his team chose to run the workshop in Nyankunde in October 2005. Heads of the army and police were also present, plus some local government officials. I have seen a video of this workshop, witnessing the Chiefs taking the sins and wounds of their tribes to the cross.

The following day they held hands in a circle with the team, asking forgiveness for their part in the civil war and pledging friendship from then on. Within a week, the conflict was over in that region of DR Congo. Looking back, many years later, that peace has largely been maintained.

(Sadly, at the time of writing, eastern Congo is suffering greatly once again. This is not the same inter-tribal warfare as before, but rather attacks by rogue groups. The main problem is a rebel group from Uganda which appears to have an Islamist agenda, and they are killing many indiscriminately. My heart goes out to my precious friends there. I pray they will continue to be hope-bearers in their very difficult situation.)

THE IMPORTANCE OF SPIRITUAL RETREATS

The teams there faced such huge challenges and had their lives threatened constantly. *How am I going to help them to keep going?* I wondered. They needed to be strengthened and encouraged regularly.

I decided to run a retreat for the teams twice a year and was delighted when my friend Cathy, who worked with Le Rucher Ministries in Geneva, agreed to work with me. Cathy is Swiss French and an anointed counsellor, so was a great asset in French speaking DR Congo.

We both felt that the priority was to help the teams find a more intimate, loving relationship with God, so that they could be sure of their God and be able to trust Him fully. That's what meets all the deep needs of the heart.

Those retreats were such precious times. We held the first in Bunia, in very basic circumstances which we both found quite challenging, but the power of God was with us as we studied God's character from Exodus 34:5-7. This is the first time in the Bible that God clearly says, 'This is what I'm like,' and this had been life-changing for me in those courses for missionaries in North Wales.

Many began to see God in a very different light, not as a harsh dictator, but as a compassionate, loving, gracious, faithful God, slow to anger, abounding in love and faithfulness, maintaining love to thousands, and forgiving wickedness, rebellion and sin. He cares and is concerned about the most intimate details of our lives. Consequently they insisted on having plenty of time to repent of their misunderstanding and misrepresentation of God as Christian leaders.

When I returned at a later date, Daniel remarked that, next to his Christian conversion, this teaching had been the most life-challenging for him. It had changed his attitude to God, his church and even his enemies.

We also looked at Job 39:1-2 that tells of God counting the days before a mountain goat and a doe give birth to their young. How much more with every son of Adam and daughter of Eve? Without planning it, I heard myself say that God had unconditionally loved even the vilest members of the militia since they were in their mother's womb. 'What?!' asked someone, 'You mean God even loves the militia?! If that's the case, we'll have to love them too!'

REACHING THE MILITIA

Very soon after this retreat, the DR Congo team received an invitation from some militia leaders. 'We are tired of fighting,' they said, 'and we have been sending spies into your workshops. You have the medicine that we need. Please would you run the workshop just for the militia, but they must be from both sides of the conflict.'

With impeccable timing, God had just been preparing their hearts for this, so the team agreed and it was a most challenging workshop. During the first day, which focuses on God's character, they were rowdy and abusive toward each other, but by the end of the day they were calming down, saying they had never heard anything like this before.

During the second day, taking their sin and pain to the cross, they were wailing loudly, even confessing cannibalism. One of the beliefs of sorcery is that eating certain human body parts protects them from bullets. (This stuff is real. I have heard stories of bullets bouncing off such people. We are so ignorant of these things in the West.)

When they got to the King's Table at the end, they wanted to bring hundreds more of their fellow militia. By now, *many* hundreds of the militia have gone through the workshops and repented of their crimes. Choirs have been formed of members of the militia composing and singing songs of repentance.

Even the two men who started the war in northeastern D R Congo have now become dear friends and are among the most effective evangelists in the region. It all started when Joel (Lendu), who was the chief sorcerer in the region, chased Nicholas (Hema) off his property. Because of pre-existing prejudice and hatred, a civil war had begun within days, predominantly between Joel's and Nicholas' tribes and lasted for 10 years. Joel and Nicholas became leaders of opposing militia groups and were responsible for the deaths of many.

Joel was the first to encounter God in a workshop and repented of all his sorcery. No one is too difficult for God's grace to reach. Cathy and I had the privilege of joining a march of repentance by former members of the militia through the town of Bunia, waving Jesus flags and singing songs of repentance. Joel was on that march but I didn't know him then. Some time later he became convicted that he had to go to find Nicholas and ask his forgiveness. He may kill me, he thought, and he would have every right to do so. But it's the right thing to do and I must go.

As he approached Nicholas' home, Nicholas saw him coming and exclaimed, 'One month ago I was in a workshop and I put everything on the cross. I already forgave you!'

I have seen a video of them testifying together in markets and villages and people kneeling in repentance in response to their message. They are now part of the reconciliation team.

BEING REFRESHED IN UGANDA

Cathy and I felt we needed to get the team out of the conflict area to a beautiful, restful place, where they could breathe freely and relax. They suggested a lovely campsite in southern Uganda on the shores of Lake Bunyoni, which was within a day's journey by road from Beni. The teams from the different regions could come down to Beni and then travel there together.

Cathy and I travelled down from Kampala by bus. Two breakdowns on the way left us stranded by the roadside until another bus picked us up. But it was worth it. We had several memorable retreats there and they were such joyful times. The campsite staff would erect a tent for us on the hillside overlooking the lake where we could hold our meetings. Even having a boat-ride in small rowing boats was a huge treat for them.

In one retreat, we were encouraging the teams to stand as fathers to offer the hug of the Heavenly Father. They were a bit reluctant, feeling inadequate for such an awesome task, so we decided to have a practice time. We asked the men to stand in front, two or three at a time, and we would come to them for a hug and they would speak to us whatever words of affirmation they believed the Heavenly Father wanted to speak to us. It was a practice, but it was also for real.

During this time, one of the wives saw a vision of the hem of a magnificent Robe descending and hovering over us. Another brother heard indescribably beautiful singing, such as he had never heard on earth, coming closer and closer. I was amazed, as I'm not very sensitive to such things, and praised God for revealing His presence to them.

On hearing the dinner bell sounding from the restaurant higher up the hillside, we left the tent. The restaurant staff came running towards us, 'Whatever was happening in there?'

they asked. 'We could feel the love of God reaching out towards us from there!' Wow! This was a secular campsite. 'We always look forward to your group coming,' they said, 'because you bring something good here.'

In another retreat, we used the Biblical symbol of marriage to explore the intimate relationship God desires to have with us. We had already looked at how our experience with our earthly fathers could block us from experiencing God as a loving Father. Now we looked at how our experience of our marriages could be blocking us from true intimacy with God. Witnessing the lack of visible intimate affection between my parents had been difficult for me and, in the past, I believe had hindered me from being comfortable in an intimate relationship with God.

Asking God for help as to how to approach this, I was led to Colossians 3:12-14. I asked them what their marriages would look like if the qualities listed in these verses – compassion, kindness, humility, gentleness, patience, forgiveness, love – were to be evident in their marriages. They were shocked. 'You need to give us time to repent now,' they said. 'None of these qualities are there!'

This led to a heartfelt time of crying out to God for mercy and the power to change things. On a later visit, it was thrilling to hear many testimonies of transformed family life.

I was shocked when one of the leaders on another retreat said, 'I come from the most despised family, in the most despised tribe, in the most despised region, in the most despised country, in the most despised continent.' It became clear that God also wanted to deal with the problem of shame.

We are told in Ephesians 6:14 to wear the belt of truth to protect against our spiritual enemy and, if we believe lies about our self-worth, there is a gap in our armour and we are vulnerable to the enemy's attack. I was concerned for them – they were on the frontline and were risking their lives constantly.

So we studied Psalm 69:7 *'For I endure scorn for your sake and shame covers my face'* – a prophetic verse about the cross where shame covered Jesus' face for our sake. Because of this, Psalm 34:5 can also be true of us. *'Those who look to him are radiant; their faces are never covered with shame'.*

We then held another Cross Session simply to deal with the various shame issues in our lives. Some spoke of the shame of not having the opportunity to be properly educated, others of the shame of poverty, past sins and so on, and then it was all nailed to the cross. It was a meaningful time and the joyful dancing which followed was unforgettable.

I learnt so much from this team and cannot honour them enough. They taught me so much, especially about persevering and trusting God in very difficult circumstances and the absolute priority of prayer. Also, I was privileged to witness miraculous, physical healings as the team, in humble but confident faith, exercised their spiritual authority. But not everyone was healed and there's always mystery there. However, I saw far more miraculous healing in Africa than I do in the West. They are so much more aware of the spiritual realm than we are. Having dealt with the dark side of the spiritual realm before coming to Jesus, they had no difficulty in believing how much more Jesus could do.

By the time we held a 10th anniversary celebration of the ministry in 2014, they estimated the number of people who had been deeply impacted at around 2 million. And over 2,000 unbelievers had become committed Christians, even including sorcerers and witchdoctors. To God be all the glory.

Chapter Twenty-one

AND TO KENYA

Kenya was considered to be a peaceful, stable country, free from the tribal tensions experienced in many other African countries. How could such massacres happen there? In the wake of disputed elections in December 2007/January 2008, the country was ripped apart by violence.

We were asked by the Anglican Church in Kenya to present our ministry approach, so Joseph went across from Rwanda to meet various church leaders.

Of all the leaders present, the ones who responded most enthusiastically were representatives of the Mothers' Union. 'We can run with this. Come and conduct the workshops for us and train us to run them.'

(The Mothers' Union is a powerful organisation in the Anglican church in Africa. With a membership of 450,000 in Kenya, it has a vital role in providing Social Services.)

I went to Kenya shortly afterwards with Rwandan and Congolese brothers. Relations between Rwanda and DR Congo were not so good at the time and we wanted to demonstrate the unity that Jesus can bring. Also, as a British person, I deeply regretted the way we had dominated and sinned against the Kenyans when we colonised Kenya. I was shocked to discover that one of the architects of apartheid in South Africa stated that they had learnt apartheid by the way we British behaved in Kenya. So I was eager for the opportunity to ask forgiveness as a British citizen.

The first workshops were attended by members of the Mothers' Union. From the start they were so responsive and were repenting that most people learn prejudice at their mother's knee. They began to realise that they had played a significant role in creating divisions in Kenya. Identifying the prejudices and realising their awful power to create conflict is a key teaching in our workshop.

TENSE WORKSHOPS

Those early workshops in Kenya were among the most tense I had ever experienced. A Christian ministry in Naivasha had kindly offered to host us in their premises. I well remember ladies waiting outside the venue in Naivasha, afraid to come in. They were afraid that they might be killed if someone of a different tribe was also attending, especially if they had to share the same sleeping quarters. This was the condition of Kenya at that time, with many being very traumatised.

But once again, we experienced God's faithfulness, bringing healing and forgiveness as people nailed their painful inner wounds to the cross. The King's Table at the end was always a particularly joyful time, where we could honour and celebrate *every* tribe.

At a later workshop, some men attended, having heard of the blessing experienced by the women. The tension at the beginning was great, someone even saying that the Bible supported ethnic cleansing. After the Cross Session, the atmosphere greatly improved.

On the last day, I was keen to repent as a British citizen. I had visited a Christian Kenyan living in my hometown in Wales to ask him to explain to me how the British had wounded Kenya. I discovered that we had committed many injustices during the MauMau period and that the Kikuyu especially held many things against us. (I was later to discover much more about this. The MauMau Uprising [1952-1960] was a war in the British Kenya Colony [1920-1963] between the Kenya Land and Freedom Army [KLFA], also known as MauMau, and the British authorities.)

I asked the oldest Kikuyu participant to step forward and began to wash his feet, seeking to come in the opposite spirit to the dominating spirit with which we had colonised Kenya. I began to confess the things I had learnt and he was very moved by this. 'So you know! You know! But it's OK. Don't upset yourself. It's OK. I forgive you!' It became clear that the whole room was very moved. To my surprise and joy, they then began to ask forgiveness of one another as different tribes, crossing the room to embrace one another. This went on for some time.

Before departing on the final morning, several wanted to testify. The old man whose feet I had washed, jumped up, saying, 'You didn't know whose feet you were washing yesterday. I fought the British during the MauMau time. And in this recent violence, I was training the youth to kill. My nickname was always "Hard Rock". But today I have a new heart. Who would have believed I could get a new heart at the age of 79!' He started jumping up and down for joy! He then made a commitment that he would go home to teach the youth the ways of peace. We later heard that he had done this.

Washing the feet of a former
Mau Mau fighter

We heard many very encouraging and moving testimonies. I was shocked when one elderly man said that he had been afraid of coming to the workshop – afraid that he might kill someone! He said that, as a Kikuyu, he hated the Kalenjin so much that if he met one in the workshop, he would surely kill him. (I'm so glad I didn't know that at the beginning.) When we put people into small intertribal groups for the Cross Session, unknowingly we had put him with a Kalenjin. But it was God's leading. Instead of killing him, they shared their hearts together, wept together and went to the cross together.

In the middle of that session, he took out his mobile phone and called his wife. 'You'll never believe what I've just done! I have shared my heart with a Kalenjin and shared even more deeply than I would with a fellow Kikuyu!' He later phoned the Kalenjin chief in his locality, to say that in the previous hour, his heart had been radically changed. He suggested that, when he got back home, they could sit together to see how the tribes could work together to help to restore the homes that had been devastated. We heard later that this did take place.

The King's Table at the end of that workshop went on until the early hours of the morning. There was so much joy and hilarity that you could have sworn they were all drunk. But we had no alcohol at the Table. Everyone was feeding each other with goodies. I had cake shoved into my mouth so many times! As the Table celebrations came to a close, each tribe did a cultural dance around the Table and I was amazed to see the Kikuyu man who had hated Kalenjin joining in the Kalenjin dance. In the end, everyone was joining everyone else's dance, though joining the high jumping of the Maasai was a challenge!

THE DANCE OF LOVE

I was shocked when those representing the Trinity at the start of a workshop started *dancing*. But then I got excited, as the whole room erupted in joy as they joined the circle. And why not? Where did every culture get their desire to express themselves in dance? In Whose image were we created? The symbol became so much richer – the Godhead inviting us to join their circular dance of love. What a liberating concept. What impact could that have on our approach to evangelism?

LOCAL OWNERSHIP OF THE MESSAGE

Training local Kenyans to conduct the workshop themselves became a priority. So it was a great joy to us when they took ownership of this ministry and began to run workshops without our help. They were passionate about seeing healing in their country and they worked hard and sacrificially, seeing many respond. The predictions were that the coming elections could be even more violent than the previous ones.

The team focused their attention on the Rift Valley, which had seen the worst violence after the previous election. They not only worked with churches, but with the community, targeting the chiefs, but also the disaffected unemployed youth who tend to be recruited as members of militia groups. We believe that their work contributed to the next elections being peaceful, and thank God for this. The work in Kenya has developed greatly by now and they have their own community-based organisation called 'Way of Peace'.

However, my work in Kenya was not over. I was invited by the national team to attend a peace rally that was being held in Eldoret, where the violence had been particularly severe. 'Please would you repent and wash feet?' they begged. 'This could have such a great impact.' So they lined up several key local leaders so that I could wash their feet after I had made a public confession of Britain's sins in Kenya. This was then recorded on the local media.

AND TO KENYA

REPENTING FOR THE SCRAMBLE FOR AFRICA

Some years before this, intercessors in the UK, France and Germany had been praying together for revival in Europe and wondered why their prayers were not being answered. As they sought God about this, they were led to 1 Samuel 21, where King David asks God why there was famine in the land. He was told that it was because of their sin against the Gibeonites.

'So, who are our Gibeonites?' they wondered. It soon became clear – Africa. Europe's sin against Africa was huge! The so-called Scramble for Africa culminated in a three-month long conference held in Berlin in 1884, during which representatives from 13 Western nations drew lines on a map of Africa, squabbling about who would own what. No African was present, or even consulted. Lines were drawn right through people groups who belonged together, while people groups who had nothing in common were joined together. Those artificial boundaries are still causing problems to this day.

The intercessors believed God was leading them to arrange a prophetic re-enactment of that conference, again in Berlin. Representatives of all the original participating countries would be invited, but this time they would also invite representatives from as many African countries as could get visas to come. This took place in November 2005 and I had the great privilege of attending.

It was an event I will never forget. Many tears were shed, as each country made its own confession of wrong towards Africa. Whilst we prepared our lists, the Africans insisted on identifying their own need of repentance such as for idolatry, tribal warfare, unjust brutal chiefs, and then asked if they could go first. They wanted clean hearts to receive our repentance.

After Europe and the US had repented, the Africans responded one country at a time, and everyone forgave us and prayed a blessing on us. It was so humbling. They also said it would be good if this could be done in their own countries. It became known as the Europe Africa Reconciliation Process.

TAKING OUR REPENTANCE TO KENYA

During many workshops in Kenya, I had witnessed that a British repentance would break the ice, enabling the Kenyans to start repenting towards one another. So I was eager to see a British repentance happening on a national level before the next elections there.

I invited some of the people who had been at the Berlin gathering in 2005 to come to Kenya. Hudson Mukunza, who led the Kenya House of Prayer at that time and who had also been in Berlin, warmly welcomed the idea. So in July 2012, five of us from the UK went to Kenya and another British person working there joined us too.

Before going, I had read 'Britain's Gulag – the Brutal End of Empire in Kenya' by Caroline Elkins. It is the hardest book I've ever read. The description of the concentration camps we created there in the 1950s and the barbaric torture methods we employed broke my heart. It's true that a few dozen White settlers were killed, but we killed hundreds of thousands of Kikuyu. I kept putting the book down, feeling that I couldn't bear it anymore, but knew I had to read it all if I was going there to repent.

It was another unforgettable event, with many tears. The Kenyans first took us to a site where early Scottish Presbyterian missionaries to Kenya had been massacred. A public meeting was held there, with deep repentance from the Kenyans. They insisted they do this before receiving our repentance.

Then we held meetings in Nairobi to convey our deepest repentance for what our country had done, as well as speaking on radio and television, confessing our wrongs. People meeting us on the street stopped us to thank us, having seen the TV programme or heard it on the radio. 'Every member of our family was in tears,' they said. 'This is healing us!'

We visited a massacre site and met survivors from the concentration camps. We washed their feet and symbolically gave them some British soil to signify our desire to give them back their own land. They were all incredibly merciful and forgave us.

Very shortly after we returned, the British government acknowledged for the first time Britain's gross wrongdoing in Kenya and even offered to pay compensation to survivors of the concentration camps. We have an enormous privilege as believers, to open up the way in the spiritual realm so that sometimes even politicians can follow. This is not the only time we have seen this happen.

Chapter Twenty-two

AND TO THE WORLD…

'We have heard about the blessing in Rwanda. We also need healing and reconciliation in this country. Can you please come here and help us?' Invitations started coming in from Côte d'Ivoire, Zimbabwe, Sri Lanka, Myanmar…

Would a message that had reached people in Africa also work for Asia? I went into each of these countries taking with me people from different countries who had already been trained, and saw God at work there too. But we soon realised that we could not go everywhere in one lifetime. There was so much need in the world for healing and reconciliation, so we began to think about further ways to multiply the ministry.

It was Joseph who first thought of running an International School of Reconciliation in Rwanda. 'Instead of us trying to go to the world, let the world come to us!' he suggested. They were renting a property in an attractive, peaceful setting that could easily house delegates from different countries. It would mean different cultures having to share accommodation, but that would be a significant part of the learning experience.

INTERNATIONAL SCHOOL OF RECONCILIATION

The first School was held in January 2012 with help from Le Rucher Ministries in Geneva. By this time, some of the Le Rucher staff were helping us by conducting other training workshops as a follow-on from our workshop.

Our reconciliation workshops are not the end of the story – they are just the beginning. Once people's hearts and relationships have been healed, they need to work together to restore the community. Reconciliation needs a practical expression. Unless we live out our reconciliation, it is meaningless.

So Renee Schudel began to conduct workshops on the Biblical basis of community development, with the aim of changing people's thinking from passivity and resignation to the belief that they could do something creative to bring about change. It was so moving and encouraging to hear of communities beginning to work together on simple initiatives using the resources they already had. This was especially effective if former perpetrators and survivors could work together. This is now happening in many places.

Where there is conflict, community development programmes without reconciliation can be a waste of effort and money, as conflict can destroy it all very quickly.

Erik Spruyt, the director of Le Rucher Ministries, also conducted teachings on Leadership and on Member Care – the care of Christian workers. In the first School, we tried to give equal time and emphasis to each aspect – reconciliation, community development, leadership and member care. Now, however, the focus is mainly on healing and reconciliation, aiming to invest in the participants as much as possible so that they can take the HWEC workshop to their own countries, but also giving a little time to the other aspects. At the time of writing (2021) we are planning our 7th School.

It was only after we had started running these Schools that I remembered the Scripture from Isaiah 60:1-3 that God had given me in the early days of my visits to Rwanda: *'Nations will come to your light…'* And now it is happening.

While we had delegates coming from many different countries and continents, it was disappointing that not all had gone home to begin the ministry in their own settings. So we tried to encourage people to come as small teams of two or three people, so that they would be more likely to start working together on their return.

We are thrilled, nevertheless, that some individuals did go home to start running workshops and have done an amazing job, far exceeding our expectations. Thomas Green, who was mentioned earlier in chapter 15, was sent to the School by EFICOR, a Christian relief and development organisation, in India. Since returning, Thomas has conducted many, many workshops in northeast India, with very encouraging results.

Joe Mulombo came to the School from Kinshasa, DR Congo, a shy, quiet, unassuming man. Amazingly, on his own, he has conducted many workshops in the Kinshasa area and even in Congo Brazzaville, the neighbouring country. God is full of surprises.

At the end of the School, we offer an optional practical training experience, where participants can go with a mentor to a university or a village in Rwanda and run the workshop themselves. Because this is a real-life situation, they are often very nervous, sometimes with former perpetrators and survivors attending the same workshop for the first time. But God has been so faithful. He has used them in their weakness to achieve His purposes and they have witnessed miracles, much to their amazement.

In one School, a team working in a rural village witnessed the real live reconciliation between a Tutsi lady who had lost many relatives in the genocide and the Hutu man who killed them. They saw her great pain – she almost collapsed as she struggled to take her pain to the cross and had to be helped to reach it. But they also saw the two of them embrace after the perpetrator repented. Since then, they have received photos on their mobile phones of the lady inviting the perpetrator to meet her family and the ensuing reconciliation. Clearly this experience has greatly increased their confidence to go back and work as reconcilers in their own countries.

The first few Schools in Rwanda were bilingual English and French, but there is now a Francophone Regional School, being held in Côte d'Ivoire, West Africa. So now the Rwandan International School is in English only.

OTHER DOORS OPEN UNEXPECTEDLY

Sometimes doors opening to multiply the ministry have come in unusual and unexpected ways. In February 2015, I was invited to share one afternoon's seminar with a Mennonite lady on the theme of reconciliation, both of us sharing our own approach. It was at an international conference on Member Care (Care of Missionaries) to be held in Antalya, Turkey, and I would have 45 minutes to give a presentation.

I was very uncertain – should I go all that way to speak for 45 minutes in a conference that was not even on reconciliation? I am so blessed to have an advisory covering group to which I am accountable. I have committed to submitting all invitations to them for their wisdom and guidance. They were as uncertain as I was, except for one person, Dewi Hughes, a former theological advisor to Tearfund. In a way that was uncharacteristic for him, he said that he felt certain that God was in this and that I should go.

It did indeed turn out to be a divine appointment. In the 45-minute seminar I met George De Vuyst, an American working with Resonate Global Mission, who had lived in Ukraine for many years. 'We need this ministry in Ukraine!' he said. He ended up attending our next International School of Reconciliation in Rwanda and then invited the ministry to Ukraine.

By now, a team of Ukrainian nationals has been trained and have gone on to conduct several workshops very near the frontline of combat in eastern Ukraine. At the end of the workshop, they have witnessed Ukrainians and Russians being able to bless one another. This is nothing short of a miracle.

We have also conducted a number of Regional Schools there, bilingual English and Russian, reaching out to the whole ex-Soviet bloc. We call it the 'Eurasian School of Reconciliation' and have received participants from sensitive countries.

In addition, George soon became an invaluable member of the international teaching team, and spends many, many hours helping with the revising of our workshop materials.

Putting flowers in the ashes in Ukraine

At that same conference in Turkey, I met a Dutch lady working in Egypt and through her the door opened to work in the Middle East. By now we have conducted two workshops and one training event in Egypt, which have been attended by people from neighbouring countries as well as Egyptians, some of them being refugees. I have always had a heart for refugees, so this is an answer to prayer. Two Egyptian couples helped me conduct the last workshop and I was so impressed by their quality as facilitators and teachers. If I hadn't gone to Turkey…

In the summer of 2018, I received an email from an American businessman working in Macedonia. He was the leader of the Balkan Call Prayer Network and he requested a Skype call with me. He said someone had given him a copy of my HWEC teaching book and he believed this was the message that was needed in the Balkans. He asked me to speak at their next Prayer conference in Kosovo in November.

I was very puzzled so during the Skype call, I enquired who had given him my teaching book. We hadn't printed the book for several years. (We are continually seeking to improve it, so we keep it online for anyone to download freely.)

He said a lady from South Africa who had moved there to live had done so. I remembered her – I had met her once at the home of my friends in South Africa who were leading the team at that time. She'd attended the workshop they had conducted, and was about to leave to work as a missionary in Sudan. Later, missionaries had had to leave Sudan and I had no more news of her. Apparently she had met a Dutchman at a conference in Germany and they both felt called to move to Macedonia.

When I heard this, I felt it had God's fingerprints all over it. This gave me the confidence to go to the Balkans to see if a door for the ministry would open there. The history of conflict in the Balkans is appalling and so complex that I would never have chosen it myself. Dr Derek Munday, who chairs my advisory covering group, accompanied me to Kosovo and we had a very moving and significant conference.

Two people approached me at the end saying that they would like to be trained to run the HWEC workshop as their nations desperately needed it. One was Pastor Venco Nakov from Macedonia and the other was Georgia from Greece, two nations who were then in conflict with each other. So I invited them both to accompany me to the workshop and training to be held in Hungary in February 2019.

Later, an invitation came to conduct the HWEC workshop in Macedonia, at Lake Prespa, which borders Greece and Albania, as well as Macedonia. The hope was that there would be some healing in the relationship between Greece and Macedonia. Neither side, however, was keen to attend. The conflict was still very raw. So the main participants were the team who led the Balkan Call Prayer Network. Georgia brought her Serbian husband and three adult children and a friend. They were the only ones from Greece. Pastor Venco Nakov brought his Bulgarian wife and some others attended from Macedonia, including both ex-pats and locals.

A Serbian wearing the Holy Nation robe in North Macedonia

There were some tense moments, especially over the name of Macedonia, officially now called North Macedonia. The two presidents had agreed on that name, but many people in both countries felt they had been betrayed by their presidents. One lady even threatened to leave after the first evening because I called the country North Macedonia.

For me, the highlight of the workshop was during the repentance time, when the Greeks and Macedonians joined in a big circular bear-hug! The local team are now interested in taking the ministry forward, hopefully eventually involving all the Balkan countries.

At the time of writing (2021), doors appear to be opening for the workshop to be invited to North and South America. That's exciting!

OTHER FAITHS?

I have been asked several times if I would consider adapting the HWEC workshop to make it suitable for other faiths. We have prayed and discussed much about this and have come to the conclusion that, although people of other faiths are very welcome to attend, we should not change the content of the workshop.

We believe that the Biblical outline of the workshop is crucial. Starting with the Trinity is foundational – that's why we were created and God's desire is that we will join the circle of loving unity in diversity. Understanding the role of the Thief in our nations is so important, and most important of all is seeing the death of Jesus on the cross as the pivotal point in human history where this world's wrongs are dealt with. He is the only sin-bearer and pain-bearer, the only one who can relieve our burdened, broken hearts.

Having said that, we have had people of other faiths attending our workshops and, as far as I'm aware, there has never been an objection to our approach. In fact, people seem to have genuinely appreciated it.

In Sri Lanka, we had to have three-way translation because of needing to work in Tamil, Sinhala and English. That was quite a challenge, especially when we received the wrong language through our headsets.

It was a shock to us as a team to discover that the translators were not Christians. They were Hindu, Buddhist and I think one was a Muslim. The percentage of Christians in Sri Lanka is very low, so they did not have many with the skills to do simultaneous translation. How on earth can they translate a Biblical workshop, we wondered, especially when the Hindu translator spoke of 'the gods' instead of God? But the participants assured us that they understood what was meant.

Following the session on God's Response to Human Suffering describing Jesus as our sin- and pain-bearer, one elderly translator approached us. 'Being here is a most wonderful experience,' he said. 'I have never heard such words before! I am a Hindu, but would you please permit me to put my pain on the cross too?' We assured him that the death of Jesus on the cross took place because God so loved the *world*. Of course, he was welcome.

Another Buddhist translator, after hearing Joseph from Rwanda teach on 'Standing in the Gap' to repent for your people group, exclaimed, 'Wow! That was amazing!'

Muslims have also loved this workshop. An Imam (a senior leader within Islam) in Rwanda attended a workshop and participated in the feedback time each morning. The first day he had been very intrigued by the focus on God's heart and character – that everything is not His will and He weeps over the brokenness of our world, but is able to redeem it.

On the last morning he admitted that when he saw the cross, he knew he could not participate in that activity as a Muslim Imam. But he had watched intently and noticed that people approached the cross looking burdened. 'But when they left, they were free!' he said. 'And I was jealous. Maybe you didn't notice that at the end I very quickly went to the cross and nailed my paper there and prayed to Allah.'

Amazingly, later that day, having listened to many asking forgiveness of one another, he stood up and said he felt he needed to ask forgiveness as a Muslim because they had not always treated Christians well. Later, on hearing this report, I asked the leader of the local team who had conducted this workshop how he had been able to persuade the Imam to attend. 'Oh, I've been befriending him for a long time,' he said. That's the key.

When the team in DR Congo flew to Central African Republic to conduct the workshop, several Muslims attended, including at least one Imam. They all loved the teaching. I asked Daniel if they had changed anything in their approach and he assured me they had not. When the team returned a few months later to do a follow-up, the Imam was there, beaming. 'I have been teaching your stuff everywhere!' he said.

The Imam said that the teaching he loved the most was about becoming a citizen of the Holy Nation. Daniel was a bit puzzled and said, 'But we said that one becomes a citizen of the Holy Nation by putting their trust in Jesus.' 'I know,' he responded. 'That's what I've been telling everyone!'

So we have learnt not to be afraid of inviting people from other faiths, but to make it clear that this is a Biblical workshop.

There are many secular organisations (and some Christian ones that use a secular approach) teaching on reconciliation in places of conflict. Reconciliation is the *fruit* of our workshops, not the content. We never 'teach' on reconciliation. But we have discovered that when people encounter God personally, have received a revelation of His heart, and have been able to give Him all their pain and anger, reconciliation is usually the outcome.

I keep hearing people saying how different our workshop is from the others on offer these days. This always puzzled me and I wondered what was so different. Daniel in DR Congo explained: 'All the way through this workshop, you are connecting us to the heart of God and He then changes our hearts.' That's something I am very happy to continue doing.

MAKING RECONCILIATION ALBUMS

Some years ago, I was introduced to the English musician Dave Bankhead who seeks to bring about reconciliation through music. His ministry is called 'We Are One' www.weareone.org). We met for a few minutes only, but he was interested to find out more.

As a result he accompanied me to South Africa with another musician and helped to lead worship in some of our workshops. He then asked me if there was any way he could serve the work in Rwanda – was anyone singing new songs of healing and forgiveness there? When I replied in the affirmative, he suggested that maybe we could make an album of them, as that was his profession. I got excited about this idea, as did Anastase and Joseph in Rwanda.

So we held workshops for songwriters in Rwanda and out of their experience in the workshops, they were encouraged to write new songs. We then selected the best ones and later brought some good singers together to record them. What a joy that whole experience was. Coming from Wales, where we naturally sing in harmony from a young age, I so appreciate African singing and I loved helping to arrange the harmonies.

I was also able to join the choir, though I had to have written notes in front of me because there's no way I could remember all those Kinyarwanda words!

Over the next few years, we made three albums: the first in 2000 was a heart cry, 'Lord, Heal our Nation!' In 2002, we made a children's album called 'Arise and Shine', and in 2004, an album of testimonies of healing and forgiveness called 'Blessed Nation'. All these are in Kinyarwanda and are available through 'We Are One' Music. In 2005, we took a group of Rwandan children who had good English, to South Africa to join with children from a very poor township, to create the English album called 'Heal Africa.'

Since then Dave has helped to make similar albums in Burundi, Kenya and Côte d'Ivoire. I wasn't involved in their making, but I rejoice in the part they have played to bring more healing to those nations.

FURTHER MULTIPLICATION

For many years, the workshop has been called Healing the Wounds of Ethnic Conflict (HWEC). However, some people have told us that, while their countries also need reconciliation, it isn't really an ethnic problem. So we have now changed the name to Healing Hearts, Transforming Nations (HHTN) and slightly modified the content to broaden the subject so that, hopefully, it will appeal to a wider audience. The only way to transform a nation is first to heal hearts.

We are still learning and constantly seeking to improve the material. The teaching book is not the final revelation on any subject, it is just the beginning. There's so much more to learn about God and His ways. Even the apostle Paul, who had experienced so many supernatural revelations, said he only knew in part (1 Corinthians 13:12).

By now the HHTN teaching book has been translated into many languages, with more being planned. We are happy for this to be spread as widely as possible and people are free to adapt the presentation of the material to their own cultures. It is available online to be freely downloaded. (See Appendix Two for details.)

When teams have been trained in different countries, we don't give them our name and we don't seek to have any control over them. We prayerfully trust them to the Holy Spirit. Other Regional Schools of Reconciliation are being conducted or planned in various parts of the world, run by an ever-increasing team of international facilitators. I am awestruck at how God continues to 'multiply loaves and fishes'.

A series of 16 short videos is being prepared (2021) to motivate people to engage with the online teaching book. While filming for these videos in 2018, I was taken back to the poor church in a rural setting near Nyamata, Rwanda. This is where the first Cross Session was held and I was asked to tell that story at that very spot.

As we finished filming, a group of people from a nearby house came running towards me, calling 'Shangaaz! Shangaaz!' (Auntie! Auntie!). To my surprise, there was Pastor Venuste and others who had been in that very first workshop in 1994. They had heard that I was coming there to film. I was tightly hugged by everyone! Pastor Venuste said that God had healed his broken heart at that first meeting, and that he had been sharing the healing message ever since.

I'm so happy to say that this ministry is no longer dependent on my involvement. Enough capable people have been trained in different parts of the world who are passionate to see healing and reconciliation spread across the globe. As well as being a vital member of the international teaching team, Joseph has established his own ministry in Rwanda called Rabagirana Ministries, and now they have their own centre, which hosts the International School of Reconciliation.

Joseph with his wife Esther

The creative aspect of the workshop has also developed. Rabagirana Ministries ran the workshop for artists, who then painted pictures from their experience of it. This is a now an exhibition called The Lighthouse, which is being used to bring further understanding and hope of healing. I particularly like the creativity in their paintings included at the end of this chapter.

Jean Paul in the northwest of Rwanda ran the workshop for actors, who then formed a reconciliation drama group, spreading the message through drama.

Other ministries have grown in other countries with their own names. If I were to die tomorrow, the work would continue. And that's how it should be.

Umugambi w'Imana ku mibanire y'abantu
Wari uko twishimira ubudasa hagati y'amatsinda y'abantu, twubahiriza, duha agaciro imico y'abandi tudahuje. Urugero rwiza rw'Imibanire ihebuje ni ubumwe mu budasa twigira mu Butatu bwera bw'Imana.

Itang 1:26; Yohani 17:21-22

Iyo urebye abo mudahuje byose, ibara, igihugu wumva ubishimiye kandi ari umugisha?
" Byapfiriye he ?

God's plan for Human relationships was that there would be unity in diversity. We should seek to come together, even as we honor and celebrate each other's cultural differences, as the Father, Jesus, and Holy Spirit are the model for perfect human relationships, different and yet One.

Genesis 1:26; John 17:21 - 22

Are you happy to see people who are different from you by ethnicity, color and country as blessing?
If not, what went wrong?"

Website: www.rabagirana.org

AND TO THE WORLD...

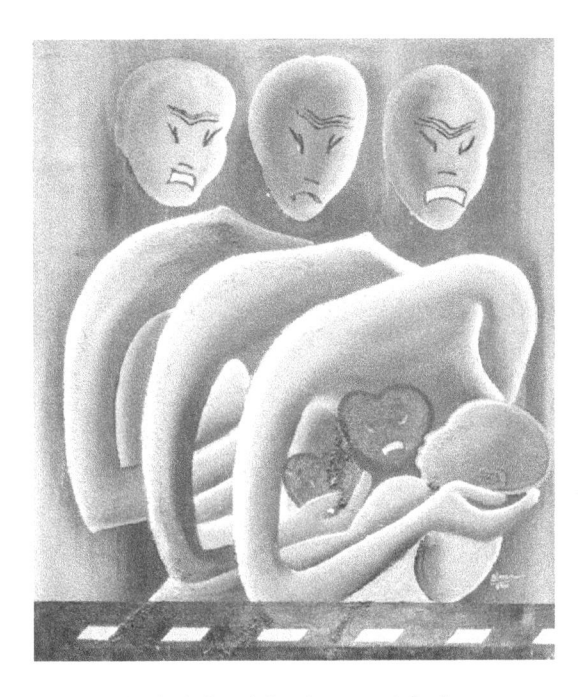

**Gushyira Itsinda ry'abantu mu gatebo kamwe
Bigira ingaruka mbi cyane. Bitera amacakubiri n'umwiryane,
byangiza imibanire bigatera amakimbirane.
Abaheburayo 12:15**

Ni ibiki byaba bigutera gushyira abantu mu gatebo kamwe?
Ni izihe ngaruka bifite ku myifatire
yawe no ku mibanire yawe n'abandi?
Usabe imana ihumanure ibitekerezo byawe.

Prejudices (bitter roots) are very destructive and are
the start of all wars and divisions
Hebrews 12:15

How have your prejudices influenced your beliefs
and attitudes? What are the results?
If not, what went wrong?"
Ask God to renew your mind.

Website: www.rabagirana.org

AFTERWORD

Looking back, I am in awe of God. I can still hardly believe what we have been privileged to witness. It feels a bit like a dream – as if I'm telling someone else's story. Why on earth would God have used a totally unknown little woman from Wales to fly into the midst of that horror, to help people find healing which would then become the means of blessing many other countries?

It hasn't all been easy. There has been a cost – the spiritual opposition against this ministry is intense. The theme of reconciliation runs right through the Scriptures. The Godhead has always desired humanity to participate in their incredible loving relationship of unity in diversity – it's who They are. That's why peacemakers are called God's children. So reconciliation is hated and strongly opposed by the enemy of our souls.

The teams have paid a high price. Two team members in different countries died very suddenly of an infected insect bite. A White farmer in South Africa who was leading the work in

KwaZulu-Natal was stabbed to death by a wandering burglar who knew nothing of how much he was loved and respected in the local Black community. Another cherished Indian team member in Durban died suddenly.

Often team members returned from workshops to find sickness and major problems in their families. The enemy has tried to divide and discredit the teams, and has sometimes succeeded with those whose security was not strongly in God.

In a smaller way, there has been a cost to my health in that much travel has affected my balance and the ground is constantly rocking for me now. It doesn't bother me too much – it's amazing what the brain can get used to. It's a very small price to pay for all the miracles of God's grace that I have witnessed.

Spiritual opposition to reconciliation is inevitable. In our experience, it seems that the greater the opposition before an event, the greater the results. When encountering all kinds of difficulties beforehand, we now tend to say, 'God must be up to something good!'

It's not always easy returning from a trip to a local church whose concerns are very different. I sometimes feel as if I've come from a different planet. When I returned from a visit to Rwanda not long after the genocide, someone asked where I had been. 'To Rwanda'. 'Oh, lovely! We went to Tenerife.' (I realise now that I have never fitted into any box, but maybe this is a price pioneers have to pay. It is inevitably a lonely path. But the results are worth it.)

It hasn't all been a wave of glory for the ministry either. There have been mistakes and disappointments. Sometimes there has not been enough prayer covering. Sometimes we thought newly trained facilitators were more healed and more mature than they really were. Sometimes we did not find the right 'person of peace' (Luke 10:6) who could take the ministry forward in their location. Sometimes teams whom we have trained, have planned enthusiastically to use the workshops in their localities, but sadly it didn't come to anything, possibly because they didn't have funding. But we are an equipping ministry, not a funding one.

The need for reconciliation in the world is so great that, sometimes, as the ministry has grown rapidly, we have focused on the work and neglected caring for and building up the individuals and teams. Some have fallen into serious sin. Some marriages have broken. But there has also been restoration of some relationships in answer to persevering prayer.

Because of the history of European abuses in Africa, whenever I land there, as a white-skinned person, I represent the oppressor. There's no getting around that. I have to accept my whiteness and seek to live in the opposite spirit. Although I have tried my hardest not to replicate the wrong attitudes and actions of white-skinned people in Africa, it is still a steep learning curve. I know I have made mistakes and have unintentionally wounded people. Racism is so much a part of the White identity that we often don't realise we are being offensive. In it all, I have found an amazing quality of mercy in Africa, as well as a readiness to forgive, that has so much to teach us in the West.

I was once told that I am an 'organisational nightmare.' It's true that I have little understanding of organisational structures and practices. I tend to think, 'What's the right thing to do now? Well, let's just do it.' without considering what that might mean to the organisation. I'm sure I have not been easy to work with within any organisational structure. Yet God has been so merciful.

In spite of everything, it has been worth it all. Those who have taken seriously the call to become reconcilers have achieved amazing results. Some of our statistics show that millions of people have now been impacted by this teaching. God's promises to me before I left for Rwanda the first time have come true, and are still coming true today. He can still multiply insignificant offerings like the loaves and fishes.

THE BLESSINGS OF TEAMWORK

There have been lessons learnt along the way. I have learnt that working in cross-cultural teams is a blessing (even if sometimes a challenge!). We each come with our own strengths and weaknesses, and can complement each other to produce something much richer in the end. I have been so blessed by the new creative approaches to presenting the material that others have brought into the ministry and I have learnt so much from them. We can also model the reconciliation which our hearts are desiring to see.

VALUES

As we have journeyed together over the years, we have developed values by which we work. The greatest is **love** and it should be our only motivation. The success of the workshop depends on everyone leaving it feeling loved, accepted and valued. The next is **hope**. It is essential that we facilitators are hope-bearers. Unless we have hope, we have nothing to offer.

But from where do we get our hope? Isaiah 11, a prophetic chapter about Jesus who would come as an amazing peacemaker enabling the most unlikely partners to live happily together, tells us in verse 3 that *'He will not judge by what he sees with his eyes, or by what he hears with his ears.'* Jesus got His hope directly from His Heavenly Father, as we see clearly in John's Gospel. We won't get our hope from the media! Or from the circumstances in our nations. We, too, need to get our hope directly from God and be people who are 'overflowing with hope' (Romans 15:13) so that those around us can share it.

We also have to have the courage to be radically honest and transparent, willing to make ourselves vulnerable by sharing our weaknesses and struggles, even when it is totally countercultural to do so. Rwanda is a strong honour/shame culture where many wear a 'mask' as the safest way to survive. Trust does not come easily. I now understand more of why the work began in Rwanda. If we could see God working miracles in such a difficult situation, we could be confident that He could do this anywhere.

We have chosen to be generous with the material. It's God's gift and it's for everyone. We have therefore been willing to train and equip other organisations so that the message can be spread as widely as possible. We have no desire to build an empire!

PRAYER

I would not dare to go anywhere to run this workshop if I didn't know there were many people praying. This prayer cover is absolutely essential. I thank God for hundreds who asked to receive my prayer update so that they could support me in prayer. Reconciliation is a spiritual battle. The workshop schedule is intense and the time we can allocate as a team to pray is often short, so we rely on the intercession of many supporters in different parts of the world. Sometimes, too, when the situation became very tense within a workshop, we stopped and prayed and this has led to a breakthrough.

HANDLING THE PAIN

I have often been asked how I handle all the pain and the stories of atrocities I hear. Isn't it all too overwhelming? Doesn't it get me down? Yes, there certainly is that danger. I think the life-saver for me is discovering Jesus as our pain-bearer.

I have had to learn to off-load it onto Jesus, preferably as soon as I hear it. Sometimes it is hard to get images out of my mind and I have to pour that pain into Jesus' heart. He is the world's Saviour, not us. Times of debriefing with especially trained counsellors have been very helpful in that regard.

Refusing to carry the responsibility for people's healing and instead giving it to Jesus is the key; also, focusing on the positives. What is God doing in the midst of it all? I have found He is always there. Rejoicing in the beautiful things He is doing, rather than the negative situation, is a key to holding onto hope.

AFTERWORD

BRAVERY?

'You're such a brave person doing what you do!' I have often been told this, but the fact is that I'm not a naturally brave person. I'm not an intrepid traveller. I would never consider travelling the world alone, given the choice. I don't enjoy taking risks, though I'm willing to do so where necessary. I'm not a calm, serene person in anxious situations, though I dearly wish I was. I'm not a good sleeper in strange beds. (Unlike one friend who told me that she could sleep on a washing line.) I have often asked God, 'Haven't You got the wrong person?' But the truth is that He delights in using weakness. *'God chose the weak things of the world to shame the strong'* (1 Corinthians 1:27-29). Why? *'So that no one may boast before him.'* He has designed us to work best when totally dependent on Him. I believe it's the prayers of many that have enabled me to keep going.

CONTINUING PERSONAL CHALLENGES

I always felt I was the world's worst intercessor and that this disqualified me from being used by God. And yet He still used me. I have realised that God works with each of us individually without comparing us with each other. Some are gifted as intercessors and can spend many hours in prayer. Some have a special sensitivity to the spiritual realm and are able to 'tune in' to God's voice very easily.

Once I was complaining to my pastor that I was so insensitive. Some people get off an aeroplane in a new country and immediately can sense the spiritual strongholds and dynamics in the spiritual realm. I get off an aeroplane thinking, 'This looks like an interesting place!' My pastor's wise response was, 'Thank God you don't sense things easily. Considering the places you go to, if you could sense the spiritual dynamics, you would not be able to function! Being you, you can go forward undeterred.' That was so reassuring to me.

Luke 18:7-8 has become very meaningful to me. Jesus is God's answer to those crying out for justice. God doesn't want to delay but to answer speedily. But will He find the faith required for Him to be able to intervene? Many times He has given me a gift of faith for the impossible. Short prayers of faith are what He was expecting from me, not long, intense intercession. I'm so relieved. I'm thankful for the *'all kinds of prayer'* mentioned in Ephesians 6:18.

Probably my most effective prayer, that I have used *very* often, has only one word in it: 'HELP!' I think that one meaning of the command to 'pray without ceasing' could be that we should leave the communication line with God open and live in the awareness of His Presence. There's no need to put the phone down. I remember one speaker in the Christian Union when I was a student in the medical school in Leeds, suggesting that we should not say 'Amen' at the end of our morning devotions. What a strange but wonderful thing that was – God was still there when I was eating my breakfast! We tend to use 'Amen' to mean 'Over and out' instead of its true meaning of 'So be it.'

I've also realised that we have different approaches to prayer according to our personalities and that's OK. Some are detailed people and they tend to pray very detailed prayers. Oth-

AFTERWORD

ers, like me, tend to focus on the bigger picture. We meditate on what God may be wanting to do through a particular situation and what the final desired outcome would be, and therefore tend to pray in that way. Both are good.

DEALING WITH WEAKNESSES

Whilst writing this book, I've come to understand more clearly that I've always been a natural leader – a visionary, a go-getter, a 'Let's do it' person. But my greatest weakness has been the inability to always know the difference between my good ideas and God's ideas. Because of that, I'm so thankful for the accountability I've had – first to Le Rucher Ministries in Geneva and more recently to my Healing the Nations advisory 'covering' group in the UK. They have helped me to discern God's leading, even when I've not always liked it! But it has been right.

Having recognised in myself a tendency sometimes to be impulsive, I promised God that I would not initiate anything, but let Him open the door. Every new workshop needs God's miracle-working power, so I have to know that this is His leading and His timing. And that works so much better than my striving to try to make things happen.

I have always struggled with being patient – both with God and with people. I want things to happen yesterday and I want people to get things right the first time. Yet as I look back, I see how very patient God has been with me.

I cringe as I recollect my immature behaviour of earlier years. Yet God didn't give up on me. He's had an awful lot of experience working with imperfect people. It's all He has! *Lord, make me more like You.*

Recognising my tendency to be judgmental, many years ago a YWAM leader helpfully told me, 'You are a very discerning person, and that's OK. The challenge for you is to turn discernment into intercession, not judgment.' That has been a steep learning curve for me. Another key I discovered in combating judgmentalism was intentionally seeking any opportunity to affirm and encourage. I was very challenged when a pastor's wife once told me that she always sought to 'look for the gold in the straw'.

I recognise more than ever how important it has been for me to have Gwenda as my sister. Someone once remarked to a friend, having watched us relating to each other with all its challenges, 'I don't think God could ever have used Rhiannon the way He does, if she didn't have Gwenda as a sister.' That's a profound truth. Gwenda helps to keep my feet firmly on the ground. In relating with her, I am constantly faced with my weaknesses and my humble need for God's daily grace. I am challenged to practise what I preach.

I have also learnt that my greatest strength is also my greatest weakness. Using my tongue in communication seems to be my greatest strength. But I have realised to my sadness that I can also use my tongue to judge and speak negatively about others. My ability to be spontaneous means I can sometimes speak too quickly, without first consulting my heart and brain.

Another strength is compassion for the hurting and desire to 'put things right'. I have not always responded wisely, sometimes creating dependency in those I have sought to help, and my desire to 'put things right' can sometimes turn into a desire to control, which I have learnt is not God's way.

Our weak areas remain something that the enemy can use. Why should he look for new ways? We can easily get back into the same ruts, so this is something I have to be continually watchful about. It's harder because I'm someone who can quickly see how things should be done in an effective way.

So when new colleagues are learning to teach the sessions in a workshop, my temptation is to jump in and correct when I think things are being missed out or not communicated clearly. This is obviously discouraging for them and disturbs the flow of the workshop. It's still a learning curve for me to bite my tongue and trust God with the outcome. After all, it's the Holy Spirit who is doing the work and thankfully it doesn't depend on a perfect presentation of the material.

But we could also look at this the other way round. We could say that God is able to turn our weakest points to be exactly what He can use most effectively for the work of the Kingdom. Our weakest points can actually become our greatest strengths. That's our redeeming God at work – the God who created fire lilies.

AND FINALLY, AS THE JOURNEY CONTINUES

What an incredible privilege it has been to watch the Holy Spirit at work, transforming lives. The impact of our workshops has been much wider than we ever expected. It has been like throwing a pebble into a pond and seeing the ripples moving out further and further and they are still going. The mustard seed has grown into a tree! Under local leadership, especially in Rwanda, it is now having a significant impact on many aspects of national life. We recognise that reconciliation is an on-going journey and healing is often multi-layered.

I have received far more than I have given. I have witnessed so many beautiful flowers growing out of the ashes of the devastation of conflict and injustice. I have been so enriched by seeing the beauty in many different cultures. It has been my greatest joy to see people receiving healing for the deepest of wounds and seeing dividing walls tumbling down. It has been such a privilege to witness the glory of God at work in some of the world's darkest places. In fact, it's in the darkest places that we have seen His glory the most. That gives me hope for each new tragic situation. I know that God will be there, quietly working miracles, though we don't hear these things on our media.

I remember the various impressions I had or messages that were given to me by others about what God might do in my future (as described in chapter 7). I can see now how faithful God has been in fulfilling them, though at the time I had no idea how He might do that. Yes, the work God gave me was something way beyond anything I could have imagined. Yes, He wanted to play 'an international tune' with my life. Yes, I would end up having more spiritual sons and daughters than I could ever count. The many lessons learnt, sometimes in a place of pain, have been used to bring comfort and freedom to so many. None of my experiences were wasted. That brings me great joy.

God really is a redeeming God! Isaiah 51:3 says, '*The Lord will surely comfort Zion and will look with compassion on all her ruins; he will make her deserts like Eden, her wastelands like the garden of the Lord. Joy and gladness will be found in her, thanksgiving and the sound of singing.*' What an amazing promise. Though originally written about Zion, we believers have now been 'grafted in' (Romans 11:17) and can share the inheritance. This can also be true of each one of us. God doesn't discard us in our brokenness, but heals and restores us so that we can help others to find beauty in their 'wastelands'. Receiving God's healing is vital.

We have witnessed repeatedly the wonder of Isaiah 61:4: '*They will rebuild the ancient ruins and restore the places long devas-*

tated; they will renew the ruined cities that have been devastated for generations.'* Who are 'they' who are experiencing such miracles? In Isaiah 61:1-3 we see that they are the broken ones that Jesus has healed, comforted, set free – the ones given a garment of praise instead of a spirit of despair. Verses 1-3 are all about what Jesus will do, but then in verse 4 it changes to 'they'. We are the wounded healers, who have proved God's healing in our own lives. There's hope for us *all*.

I am now more convinced than ever about the centrality of the cross in all that we do. While conducting the HHTN workshop in Wales, I was struggling, knowing that no group was worthy to fulfil God's purposes in the nation: Welsh speakers, non-Welsh speakers and folk who had moved in from outside – we had all failed to live as God desired.

Then God reminded me of Revelation 5 – another situation where there was weeping because no one was worthy to carry out God's purposes. Then they discovered Someone who was worthy – the Lion of Judah. But when they looked at Him, what they saw was a Lamb – one that has been slain. Of course, Jesus is the only One worthy to heal our nations. He paid the full price for that on the cross. It was all included in His atoning sacrifice.

I am still learning and am finding Scriptures like Colossians 1:20 that tell us that the reconciling work of Jesus on the cross covers *everything! Really?* In 2 Corinthians 5:19, which says that God was in Christ reconciling the world to himself, the Greek word for *world* is *cosmos*. This is mind blowing. It means that what we are privileged to do with God is just a small part of a much bigger picture.

Although some might suggest adopting a non-offensive approach which would be suitable for all religions and none, there is nothing to compare with the foundational Biblical truths to heal and transform a broken world:

• the welcoming invitation to join the loving unity of the Trinity;

• the security of the embrace of the Loving Father;

• Jesus' redemptive work on the cross to take the whole tragic human condition into Himself, turning our loss into gain;

• the restored identity that is offered to us as fellow citizens in the Holy Nation, where we can honour each other and celebrate our diversity.

It's experiencing these truths that is creating miracles in millions by now. To God be all the glory.

THE SUPREMACY OF LOVE

I had always thought that, as I approached the end of my earthly journey, I would be wondering how much I had achieved. Was it enough? *What is enough?* Was my life a success? I no longer believe that achievement and success are the goal of our lives. I am realising more and more that the only thing God is interested in, is whether we have lived a life of love. If someone wanted to write something on my tombstone, I would be so happy if they felt they could simply write the two words, *'She loved'*. Nothing else matters. I so hope they would be able to do that. I must be honest: it hasn't always been the main goal of my life and I have a way to go yet.

I could re-write and summarise 1 Corinthians 13:1-3 for my situation. 'If I am recognised as an international teacher, but have not love, I am only a resounding gong or a clanging cymbal. If my ministry impacts millions of lives and I have faith to work in the most challenging places, but have not love, I am nothing.'

How I wish now that I had first heard the Gospel in a very different way – that Love Himself desired to come and take residence within me and, with other believers, progressively to transform us into the most loving people on the planet. What a difference that would have made to my understanding of the purpose of my life. Jesus said that by *this* (loving one another) people would come to believe. It's only in my 'twilight' years that this is beginning to sink in.

God has clearly impressed on me that the *real* me is not my public face, but what I'm like with my nearest and dearest, in my case my sister Gwenda. Colossians 3:12-14 are an ongoing challenge. Looking back now, I suspect that, from God's perspective, loving my sister and eating 'pap' with a housemaid in her servant quarters in South Africa, were the most important things I ever did. Lord, teach me to love all your children unconditionally.

As the ministry grows, I have become aware that it must never become an idol. As Paul Oakley writes in his worship song, 'Jesus, Lover of My Soul':

> *'It's all about You, Jesus, and all this is for You,*
> *for Your glory and Your fame,*
> *It's not about me, as if You should do things my way,*
> *for You alone are God and I surrender to your ways.'*

Keeping an intimate loving relationship with God Himself must always be my priority.

I've asked God that if I ever start getting my significance from the 'success' of what I do, He must take it away from me. My goal must always be to live in the embrace of the Father and to keep that as my first love. Some years ago, I felt God was saying to me, 'Stay small (in your own eyes), cling close, then there will be no limit to what I can do.'

BEING A HOPE-BEARER

I believe this is an on-going call on my life wherever I am. How our broken world needs hope. I believe that being a hope-bearer in every situation will be a privilege and a challenge for the rest of my life. We have a solid foundation for our hope – that everything is redeemable and God can grow fire lilies out of all the world's ashes.

AND FINALLY, AS THE JOURNEY CONTINUES

'O Love that will not let me go,
I rest my weary soul in thee;
I give thee back the life I owe,
That in thine ocean depths its flow
May richer, fuller be.

O Light, that followest all my way,
I yield my flickering torch to thee.
My heart restores its borrowed ray
That in thy sunshine blaze its day
May brighter, fairer be.

O Joy that seekest me through pain
I cannot close my heart to thee;
I trace the rainbow through the rain,
And feel the promise is not vain,
That morn shall tearless be.

O Cross that liftest up my head,
I dare not ask to fly from thee;
I lay in dust life's glory dead,
And from the ground there blossoms red
Life that shall endless be.'

George Matheson, 1882

Appendix One

SUGGESTIONS FOR PERSONAL OR GROUP REFLECTION

Chapter One: The Bridge

Can you remember a moment where you found yourself in a place you never expected to be and discovered God had put you there?

Can you see ways God had been preparing you for that?

Chapter Two: Designed by a Master Craftsman

Which of your experiences as you grew up do you think formed the person you have become?

Did they lead you towards God or away from Him?

Chapter Three: Where on Earth Have I Landed?

Do you have a sense of vocation, of God's hand upon your life to lead you?

Has your sense of vocation changed over the years?

Do you know the means God uses most often to speak to you or to get your attention?

Have you struggled with the need to be in control? If so, take time to talk to God about it.

Were there any frustrations you had to try to cope with?

Chapter Four: On Being Welsh

Is your ethnic identity something you feel comfortable with, or is there some wounding or sense of superiority involved?

Is that identity more important to you than your spiritual identity? If you find this question difficult to answer, perhaps ask God to show you.

Chapter Five: Facing my Inner Struggles

What is your first inner reaction when you think of God? How do you *feel* about Him? Try to be very honest.

Is this reaction to God positive or negative? (Note: This may not be the same as your stated beliefs.)

Do you secretly see Him as the author of life's tragedies?

How could you help someone else struggling with their view of God?

Chapter Six: Discovering God as the Redeemer of Everything

Ask the Holy Spirit to reveal any ways in which you might have become offended at God.

Can you talk to God honestly of your feelings about Him?

Can you ask Him where He was during your times of difficulty and pain, asking Him to show you what's in His heart for you?

Have you ever experienced something good eventually coming from a time of loss or suffering?

Chapter Seven: More Experiences of Preparation

How would you describe your passion?

Have you sometimes had the sense that you were destined for greater things in your life?

Can you think of experiences that have radically changed your understanding of God / life? How did that change in understanding make a practical difference to your life?

Chapter Eight: Lessons Learnt in Liberia

Has there been a situation you were reluctant to face, which has actually turned into a blessing?

If God is lovingly looking at what you will become as well as what you are now, what might He see?

What would a perfect father look like to you?

Are there any painful experiences in your life that, once healed, God could use to enable you to bless someone else who is suffering?

Chapter Nine: Invitation to Rwanda

What gives you hope?

How could you bring hope to someone else?

Chapter Ten: Meeting Christian Leaders in Kigali

Ask God to show you if there are cultural beliefs that prevent you from knowing Him better.

Is there anything that would help you to remove any 'mask' you may be hiding behind?

How might your own story of struggle bring healing to others?

Chapter Eleven: Finding Healing at the Cross

Ask God to give you a deeper understanding of the meaning of the cross.

Is there any trauma in your life for which you would like help, counsel and prayer?

Is there anything you have been carrying in your heart that you want to give to Jesus?

What would help you to pour out your pain into the heart of God? Is there something that's preventing you from doing this?

Chapter Twelve: The *Healing the Wounds of Ethnic Conflict* (HWEC) Workshop is Born

Are there signs that the church in your locality first needs healing before it can become an agent of healing for others?

Have you ever needed to persevere in the face of hindrances and discouragements? What good came out of it?

Chapter Thirteen: The HWEC Workshop Develops

Are there places you avoid or prefer not to visit because they hold painful memories?

Do you find it easier to forgive people who are far away, and harder to forgive those who are near?

Is there anyone you need to forgive who is close?

Chapter Fourteen: Multiplying the Ministry

Have you ever been prevented from doing something you really wanted to do, only to discover later that God had a better plan?

Ask the Holy Spirit to reveal any hidden prejudices that may be in your heart.

Are there any creative ways God might lead you to help form unlikely partnerships between people?

Chapter Fifteen: Finding God as a Loving Father

When you picture your heavenly Father what do you see?

How do you think He feels about you?

Ask God to show you what childhood experiences have influenced the way you see Him.

Ask Him to help you to forgive your parents for any way they may have failed you, and then run into His loving embrace. He can meet all the needs of your heart.

Chapter Sixteen: Shocking Forgiveness

Have you ever found that forgiving someone has brought you a new freedom?

Ask the Holy Spirit to reveal to you if there is anyone you might be dragging through life with a rope of unforgiveness.

Is there any way you could help mediate between people who are at enmity with each other?

Chapter Seventeen: The Challenge of Repentance

Is there anyone you might have offended, so need to ask their forgiveness and God's?

With what groups do you identify (ethnic, racial, country, gender, denomination, profession and so on?)

What sinful attitudes or actions have your group(s) been guilty of?

Are there any opportunities you could take to stand in the gap on behalf of your group?

Chapter Eighteen: Invitation to South Africa

Are there culturally creative ways you could use to reach out to people you would not normally associate with?

Chapter Nineteen: New Creative Ideas in South Africa

What can the Trinity teach you about relating to other people?

Is there a people group that has been stolen from you that you want back?

What positive comments could you make about other groups in your day-to-day conversations?

Ask God to show you if there is someone He wants you to bless, and in what way.

Chapter Twenty: The message Spreads to Congo

How might understanding more of God's character help you relate to people in a different way, especially to those you consider to be 'unlovely'?

Ask God to help you see everyone as loved unconditionally by Him.

Chapter Twenty-one: To Kenya…

How do you see the cross reconciling enemies?

Does the symbolic act of feet-washing seem meaningful to you? Have you ever taken part in this? Might there be a situation where it would be helpful?

What would be your response to an invitation from the Trinity to join in their 'dance of love'?

What opportunities can you use to invite others to join the circle?

Chapter Twenty-two: And to the World…

Can you envisage creative ways of furthering reconciliation in your country?

Are there people who could be trained to do what you are doing?

Are you working yourself out of a job?

Afterword

What do you think are your strengths and weaknesses and can you see how God has used both?

Can you recollect any promises God made to you that have now been fulfilled?

Are there 'fire lilies' growing out of any places of suffering in your life?

Ask God to show you His priorities for you in future.

Appendix Two

HEALING HEARTS, TRANSFORMING NATIONS

Please see www.HHTNglobal.org for more information about this ministry, where you will find:

- Our teaching book, *Healing Hearts, Transforming Nations* in many different languages.

- A series of 16 videos by the same name, which aims to motivate people to engage with the online teaching using testimonies and film clips from the workshops.

- A PDF which accompanies the audiobook of *Fire Lilies*, showing the pictures and diagrams.

- The book, *Jesus is our He*ro, written in 2006 by me, together with Anastase Sabamungu (Tutsi), and Joseph Nyamutera (Hutu), gives a more detailed account of the structure and fruit of the workshop.

• A document outlining the principles of healing and reconciliation for anyone considering inviting the ministry to their location.

• Information about the International School of Reconciliation in Rwanda; Eurasian School of Reconciliation; and Regional Schools, with dates of future events.

• A link to *Hope of a Thousand Hills* – a book written by Emily Bankhead, giving the history of the work in Rwanda.

Appendix Two

Healing Hearts, Transforming Nations Workshop*

Section 1: Laying the Foundation

1. God's Original Intention for Relationships
2. The Awful Power of Prejudice: Bitter Roots
3. A Restored Identity
4. The Church as an Agent of Change
5. Suffering and a God of Love
6. Knowing God as a Loving Father

Section 2: Building the Walls

7. The Thief
8. The Wounded Heart
9. God's Response to Human Suffering
10. The Cross Workshop

Section 3: Putting on the Ceiling

11. Forgiving the Offender
12. The Transforming Power of Repentance and Asking Forgiveness
13. Standing in the Gap

Section 4: Now for the Roof!

14. Pronouncing Blessings
15. Where Do We Go From Here?

* Formerly the *Healing the Wounds of Ethnic Conflict* workshop (HWEC)

Appendix Three

ACKNOWLEDEGMENTS

I am grateful to many people who have helped me get this book written and published. First, I want to thank my advisory covering group who strongly encouraged me, saying that I would be disobeying God if I didn't write a book about my story. Without this strong encouragement, I probably wouldn't have done it.

There are many more I need to thank: Sandy Waldron, whose editorial gifting and advice was a great encouragement in the early days of writing this book; Mary Munday, a close friend who is also one of the advisory covering group, and an avid reader, spent many hours going through the script over and over, giving me much useful advice; Christine Orme, a former English teacher and editor, also gave many hours to correct my grammar and suggest improvements and was a great encourager; Fawn Parish, a dear friend and author of many books, who is also the director of the International Reconciliation Coalition, also gave very valuable advice.

Martin Harrison, a friend from church and an author, has spent many hours formatting and correcting the book and preparing it for publication, and has been an invaluable asset. I cannot express how grateful I am.

My gratitude also goes out to Les Roberts, Diane Conde, Rosie Leavers and Elaine Harrison for proof reading, and to all those who have kindly read and endorsed the book.

I am also so grateful to Mark Pierce not only for designing the beautiful cover but also for reformatting this 2nd edition, and especially for the hours spent improving the graphics and the quality of the photographs.

Looking back on my life, I have so much gratitude to my parents, and to all those who have helped to shape me in many different ways, especially staff at YWAM, Nuneaton.

My gratitude to all the heroes mentioned in these stories, and in many more stories not recorded, knows no bounds. You are the ones who have made it all so worthwhile. It has been my greatest privilege to be able to serve you and learn so much from you. This is really your story.

And lastly, my greatest gratitude is to our great Redeemer Jesus, who enables us to become 'more than conquerors' whatever difficulties, challenges, and tragedies we face in our lives. He is the One who brings the beauty out of life's ashes and gives us eternal hope. May He be glorified forever.

Milton Keynes UK
Ingram Content Group UK Ltd.
UKHW051123020924
447707UK00007B/60